Praise for

IS LITERACY ENOUGH?

"Masterfully show[s] that academic success for the at-risk student can only be achieved by a scientifically grounded curriculum that takes the child from preschool to high school graduation."

—**Maggie Bruck**
Johns Hopkins Medical Institutions
Division of Child/Adolescent Psychiatry

"[Provides] timely insights about what propels children living in poverty toward academic success. [This book] studies children from age 3 through high school, noting the positive impact of language and literacy competence, and points out that this is not enough for success in middle and high school. What is necessary also is the involvement of adults, parents, or teachers supporting students' motivation and planning for academic success. A gem for educators and leaders."

—**M. Susan Burns, Ph.D.**
College of Education and Human Development
George Mason University

"Fascinating, thought provoking, and insightful. Catherine Snow, one of the world's leading scholars on literacy, and her colleagues brilliantly explain the linkages of literacy performance across the age span. This book is in a class of its own! It is a remarkable contribution to the literature on literacy achievement. It will be embraced by practitioners, policy makers, and scholars alike. Complex data sets are lucidly presented and are brought to life through engaging case studies."

—**Donald D. Deshler, Ph.D.**
University of Kansas
Center for Research on Learning

"At last, a book with data explaining why some preschoolers become high school dropouts and others academic successes."

—**Barbara R. Foorman, Ph.D.**
Florida Center for Reading Research

"Fills a gap in the information available about literacy and schooling . . . coherent and persuasive."

—**Peg Griffin, Ph.D.**
e Human Cognition
: of Communication
'alifornia–San Diego

"The information contained in this volume is both timely and extraordinarily important, and it makes a powerful case for comprehensive middle and high school reform. As the authors show, students rarely succeed in the upper grades without strong literacy skills—but literacy alone isn't enough. We must redesign our secondary schools to meet the needs of an increasingly competitive 21st century, and provide graduate students with the full range of knowledge and skills they will need to successfully meet the challenges of college and work."

—**Bob Wise**
Alliance for Excellent Education

IS LITERACY
ENOUGH?

IS LITERACY ENOUGH?

PATHWAYS TO ACADEMIC SUCCESS FOR ADOLESCENTS

by

Catherine E. Snow, Ph.D.
Harvard Graduate School of Education
Cambridge, Massachusetts

Michelle V. Porche, Ed.D.
Wellesley Centers for Women
Wellesley, Massachusetts

Patton O. Tabors, Ed.D.
Cambridge, Massachusetts

and

Stephanie Ross Harris, M.A.
Wellesley Centers for Women
Wellesley, Massachusetts

·P A U L·H·
BROOKES
PUBLISHING Co.®

Baltimore • London • Sydney

·P A U L·H·
BROOKES
PUBLISHING C⁰ ®

Paul H. Brookes Publishing Co.
Post Office Box 10624
Baltimore, Maryland 21285-0624

www.brookespublishing.com

Copyright © 2007 by Paul H. Brookes Publishing Co., Inc.
All rights reserved.

"Paul H. Brookes Publishing Co.," is a registered trademark of
Paul H. Brookes Publishing Co., Inc.

Typeset by Spearhead Global, Inc., Bear, Delaware.
Manufactured in the United States of America by
Versa Press, Inc., East Peoria, Illinois.

All of the individuals in this book have been given pseudonyms to protect their privacy,
and some identifying details have been changed.

Library of Congress Cataloging-in-Publication Data

Is literacy enough? : pathways to academic success for adolescents / by Catherine E. Snow
... [et al.].
  p.   cm.
  Includes bibliographical references and index.
  ISBN-13: 978-1-55766-914-8 (pbk.)
  ISBN-10: 1-55766-913-9 (pbk.)
  1. Reading (Secondary)—United States. 2.   Academic achievement—United States—
Longitudinal studies.   I. Snow, Catherine E.   II. Title.

LB1632.I79 2007
428.4071'2—dc22   2007005296

British Library Cataloguing in Publication data are available from the British Library.

Contents

About the Authors

Catherine E. Snow, Ph.D., Henry Lee Shattuck Professor of Education, Chair, Human Development and Psychology Department, Harvard Graduate School of Education, Larsen 313, Cambridge, MA 02138

Dr. Snow received her doctorate in psychology from McGill University and worked for several years in the linguistics department of the University of Amsterdam. Her research has focused on children's language development, literacy development, social and familial influences on literacy development, acquisition of language and literacy by children from language minority families, adolescent literacy, and the prerequisites for improving literacy instruction in middle and secondary schools. She has published several books and many articles in refereed journals and chapters in edited volumes. Snow chaired the National Research Council Committee on Preventing Reading Difficulties in Young Children; the RAND Reading Study Group, which produced the volume *Reading for Understanding: Towards an R&D Agenda*; and the National Academy of Education committee, which produced the volume *Knowledge to Support the Teaching of Reading*.

Michelle V. Porche, Ed.D., Research Scientist, Wellesley Centers for Women, Wellesley College, 106 Central Street, Cheever House, Wellesley, MA 02481

The emphasis of Dr. Porche's research at the Wellesley Centers for Women is on the study of literacy and achievement. For more than a decade, she served as a member of the research team of the Home–School Study of Language and Literacy Development. Her doctoral thesis, completed at the Harvard Graduate School of Education, focused on parent involvement and its relationship to school achievement for Home–School Study participants. Selected parts of that work appeared as the chapter "Parent Involvement as a Link between the Home and School" in *Beginning Literacy with Language: Young Children Learning at Home and in School* (edited by David K. Dickinson and Patton O. Tabors and published by Paul H. Brookes Publishing Co., 2001). Dr. Porche has also been engaged in research and evaluation of a number of literacy intervention projects from preschool to middle school aimed at children from low-income homes. In several cases, the strategies of these interventions have been informed by findings of the Home–School Study. The most notable example is Project EASE, for which she was a co-recipient of the Albert J. Harris Award in 2002 from the International Reading Association for the article "Project EASE: The Effect of a Family Literacy Project on Kindergarten Students' Early Literacy Skills" (Jordan, Snow, & Porche, 2000).

The influence of socioemotional factors is of primary interest in Dr. Porche's investigations of literacy and achievement. Her most recent work includes investigation of the impact of psychological trauma and stress on literacy development and learning, and collaboration in a study of the social-ecological and relational contexts that hinder girls' and minority youths' persistence in science, technology, engineering, and mathematics career trajectories.

Patton O. Tabors, Ed.D., Cambridge, MA 02138

Patton O. Tabors, Ed.D., retired in 2005 as Principal Research Associate at the Harvard Graduate School of Education. Prior to beginning her doctoral studies at the Harvard Graduate School of Education in 1981, Dr. Tabors was an elementary school teacher and a childbirth educator. Her doctoral studies focused on first and second language acquisition in young children. Her dissertation research described the developmental pathways of a group of young children learning English as a second language, which she later wrote about in *One Child, Two Languages: A Guide for Preschool Educators of Children Learning English as a Second Language* (published by Paul H. Brookes Publishing Co., 1997).

From 1987 until 2003, Dr. Tabors was the research coordinator of the Home–School Study of Language and Literacy Development in collaboration with Catherine E. Snow and David K. Dickinson. She is the editor, with Dickinson, of *Beginning Literacy with Language: Young Children Learning at Home and School* (Paul H. Brookes Publishing Co., 2001). During this time Dr. Tabors also directed research related to low-education and low-income mothers reading to their preschool-age children as part of the Manpower Development Research Corporation evaluations of two welfare-to-work projects—New Chance and JOBS—and she directed research for the Harvard Language Diversity Project, a subproject of the New England Research Center on Head Start Quality, directed by Dr. Dickinson. In 2000, Dr. Tabors became the principal investigator of a longitudinal project, the Early Childhood Study of Language and Literacy Development of Spanish-Speaking Children, which followed a sample of more than 300 bilingual children from preschool to second grade.

Stephanie Ross Harris, M.A., Project Associate, Wellesley Centers for Women, Wellesley College, 106 Central Street, Cheever House, Wellesley, MA, 02481

Ms. Harris has been involved in the Home–School Study of Language and Literacy Development at the Harvard Graduate School of Education since its inception. She began as Preschool Coordinator, for which she supervised and collected data in children's preschool and kindergarten classrooms. By the end of the project she was Project Director and was involved in all aspects of its administration. In between she took a 5-year hiatus to attend graduate school and then worked as a school psychologist. After the Home–School Study ended, she became a site coordinator for the Early Childhood Study of Language and Literacy Development of Spanish-Speaking Children and continues to work on research projects related to language and literacy. She is co-author, with Michelle V. Porche and Catherine E. Snow, of a chapter in the book *Adolescent Boys: Exploring Diverse Cultures of Boyhood* (New York University Press, 2004) titled, "From Preschool to Middle School: The Role of Masculinity in Low-Income Urban Adolescent Boys' Literacy Skills and Academic Achievement."

Foreword

Literacy learning, academic progress, educational aspirations, and the effectiveness of schooling are all developmental processes, ebbing and flowing through the lives of children and adolescents. And yet, research scientists rarely examine these processes longitudinally. Empirical studies over the length of an entire school year make up much of the universe of what are considered to be "long studies" in these fields—a span of observation too brief to expose and explore the natural bumpiness of learning.

In this context, it seems fair to say that *Is Literacy Enough? Pathways to Academic Success for Adolescents* offers the proverbial hen's teeth of educational science: a provocative documentation of literacy learning across the lives of more than 40 students from preschool through high school; with all of the fits and starts, hopes and dreams, promises and failures, surprises good and bad, and, sadly, the fulfilled and unfulfilled expectations that it implies.

This book is both straightforward and complex. The authors' plan is clear, but the observations and conceptions themselves show subtlety of thought and an intricacy of reasoning. Given this, there were a few things that we thought readers might want to think about before reading this singular and informative work. The results of this longitudinal study are poised uncomfortably at the juncture between the statistical analysis of groups and the lived experiences of individuals. Correlations describe the extent to which events co-occur, and they are calculated on a scale from zero to one. Few relationships are so perfect that they merit a 1.00, and coincidences occur with some frequency so that zeroes are rare, too.

Let's say two variables share a correlation of .80. That is a strong relationship, meaning the two variables frequently occur together. But even this strong a correlation is far from perfect, so there will be plenty of individual exceptions to the general pattern. Correlations show, for example, that individuals who complete college will be paid much more in their lifetimes than those without a degree. The close correlation of years of schooling and income for the group is irrefutable, but Microsoft mogul Bill Gates, the richest man in the world at the time of this book's publication, gives lie to this because he never completed college. The correlations are accurate in a case like this because they summarize what is generally true for the group, but the exceptions are true as well because the correlations aren't perfect. The Snow et al. study requires that readers simultaneously grasp the reality of both group consistency and individual exceptionality.

Something else worth thinking about is the landmark work of Helen Robinson, a pioneer in the field of reading education from the University of Chicago, who conducted similar research in the 1940s. Robinson took a very different tack than the one in this volume. She did not follow students over time and she used different measures, but her findings seem relevant and worth thinking about.

Robinson was interested in what caused reading failure in schoolchildren. She tested students on an extensive battery of measures, including assessments of sensory, perceptual, physical, linguistic, cognitive, and experiential factors. Her results were as surprising as some of the results in this book. No single malady, weakness, or limitation was sufficient to consistently prevent students from learning to read, but combinations of limiting factors could be crushing.

Students, even those growing up in poverty, often prove to be amazingly resilient, but as Snow and her colleagues reveal, much can go wrong for such students, too, and the more that goes wrong, the less likely their success. Students with weak early literacy skills may succeed later, but this depends on the availability of alternative sources of social support and individual force or motivation. Likewise, advanced literacy skills will not guarantee high school graduation, as myriad personal, social, and economic pressures can still interfere. (This is something we know about personally because one of the authors of this foreword is a high school dropout who still soldiers on without benefit of a diploma or a GED.) Only about one-third of high school dropouts leave school due to academic problems, so adequate achievement is a necessary but insufficient condition for high school success.

This book shows that students can overcome academic problems as well as some of the limitations imposed by poverty, racism, poor teaching, lack of parental academic success, and weak motivation. But it also shows that accumulations of these problems can be devastating. Clearly, if we want students to succeed (and that is a complex goal that goes far beyond the end of schooling), we need to protect them from as many risk factors as possible—including those threats that arise through their own sometimes troubling actions, beliefs, and social relationships.

Much of the recent work on literacy education has emphasized the importance of creating early success, and the idea of getting kids on track from the beginning makes great sense. However, in far too many schools, this has been misinterpreted to mean that only early literacy teaching matters. Students should be getting high-quality reading and writing instruction throughout their education, including in high school, and if they have not managed to receive the benefit of such instruction early on, that does not mean that later efforts cannot still make an important contribution to these students' lives. Ongoing, high-quality literacy instruction is not a magic bullet, of course; as this study makes so clear, there are no easy fixes, just many variables that in concert can support or undermine success. Providing substantial amounts of quality literacy and language teaching throughout students' schooling is a good idea; it is just not the *only* good idea.

One last thought: Many years ago, we read about the role of medical science in increasing life span since the 1850s. The gains in life span have been remarkable in Western societies; White males in the United States born in 1850 could expect to live only to be about 38, and White females, to about 40. Statistics were even worse for non-White individuals; as late as 1900 they, on average, only lived to be about 32. Now, average life spans are much, much longer (e.g., White women can expect to reach age 80, and non-White individuals usually live into their 60s).

What caused these dramatic improvements? According to most analyses, they are most accurately attributed to improvements in sanitation, food handling, and water purification, rather than better medical care. In fact, one pessimistic analysis attributed only 3% of the gain to all of our scientific and technological breakthroughs in medicine. That sounds bad for physicians and medical researchers, but would you give up 3% of your life? It might not sound like much within the whole picture, but it matters deeply both to individuals and populations.

Is Literacy Enough? contains some important revelations about the limits of improving reading achievement. It is clear that improving literacy in the elementary school years will not be enough to guarantee high school success. There are many other environmental and educational factors that matter, too, some measured here and some not.[1]

We think this study is correct overall, but we also anticipate the conclusions that some might draw: If improved early literacy achievement will not guarantee later academic success, why invest so much in it? Sadly, teachers' efforts too often follow their low expectations of students, and such findings could put some educators off by emphasizing the seeming hopelessness of the situation. The message they may get is "Make kids better readers and they still might get derailed."

---

[1]Critical variables not measured here include the quality and quantity of reading instruction given to these children; it is clear from the findings that the instruction they did get was not sufficiently powerful to change much for these kids. In many schools, students get less and less access to literacy instruction as they advance through the grades, and this itself could be a risk factor, particularly for those students with early difficulty. That's a problem with longitudinal studies; it is impossible to anticipate fully what patterns will be found and what additional measures would help with the consequent interpretation. The relationship between quantity and quality of teaching and the stability of student literacy performance must be followed up in future research studies.

We believe that such a conclusion would be comparable to ending medical research because of its limited impact on keeping us alive. The research presented in this book shows that there are factors beyond teachers' control that can prevent kids from succeeding in school and in life. What we have to recognize is that if there is to be any hope for students, we as educators, regardless of the parts of the process that we do not control, must do everything possible to succeed with the parts for which we are responsible. Would you give up 3% of these kids?

Timothy Shanahan, Ph.D.
Cynthia R. Shanahan, Ph.D.
Professors of Curriculum and Instruction
University of Illinois at Chicago

Preface

In 1987, Shelby Miller, then a program officer for the Ford Foundation, contacted Catherine E. Snow, a professor at the Harvard Graduate School of Education, wanting to know if she had any ideas for research related to young children's language development that could be supported by the Foundation. In response to this unusual offer, Dr. Snow and David K. Dickinson, then at Tufts University, retooled a previously unfunded proposal for a prospective longitudinal study of the language and literacy development of young children from low-income homes. The assumption of the proposal was that, although all of these children could be considered at risk for literacy difficulties, some of them would turn out to be good readers. The purpose of the study would be to differentiate factors, both at home and in preschool, that were associated with different literacy outcomes for this group of children. This was the genesis of the Home–School Study of Language and Literacy Development.

The original plan was for a relatively short-term study that would follow young children just until they started to learn to read. But researchers are always unwilling to abandon a longitudinal sample, so it eventually developed into a long-term study in which we followed the children all the way through high school. The study started with a sample of 83 3-year-old children; at its conclusion in 2003, we were still in contact with 47 of the participants, who had become adolescents verging on young adulthood.

Starting with Drs. Snow and Dickinson as co-principal investigators, the research team grew to include Patton O. Tabors as research associate, Stephanie Ross Harris as research assistant, and Michelle V. Porche, first as a graduate research assistant and then as research analyst. Continuation funding was secured from the Spencer Foundation, the Department of Health and Human Services (Head Start Grant), and the William T. Grant Foundation. In addition, the Harvard Graduate School of Education, Tufts University, and Clark University provided office space and logistical support at various times during the project. None of the research would have been possible without this support from organizations willing to take a chance that it would reap valuable insights into the academic experiences of low-income students.

The data collection process for this study was intensive, extensive, and often challenging. Families and children were recruited for the study through preschool programs serving low-income communities in the greater Boston area. We were asking families for permission to visit their children's classrooms, and to visit them in their homes as well. Although we were offering a small remuneration for the home visits, we were really asking the families to clear their schedules and let us into their lives for a morning or an afternoon each year for the first 3 years of the study and for further home visits during elementary, middle, and high school. Most of the original group of families stayed with the study through preschool, but some decided not to continue beyond the originally scheduled 3 years. As the project continued, there were some families who could not be located or who moved out of the area; other families started leaving it up to their children whether or not they wished to continue. Each year a lot of detective work went into locating and contacting families for a new round of data collection, and, in the later years, persuading reluctant adolescents that it could be fun. We were fortunate that a core group of families was always willing to keep participating.

Year after year, Drs. Snow, Dickinson, and Tabors were able to attract a talented group of research assistants to the study. These indefatigable assistants, who were undergraduate and graduate students from nearby institutions, did the detective work, made the appointments, and braved unpredictable traffic patterns to travel to homes and classrooms in order to procure the data in the form of audiotapes, assessments, and interviews. During the course of this work, these assistants learned the need for flexibility and a sense of humor in the process of actually finding families at home or teachers who were willing to have outsiders in their classrooms. There were many adventures; in one case, two home visitors drove away from a visit with their research notes on top of their car, and had to re-collect the notes from up and down a busy urban thoroughfare.

Research assistants also had the challenging task of transcribing audiotapes of mother–child interactions (including multiple readings of *The Very Hungry Caterpillar*); family mealtimes; and mother, teacher, and student interviews, as well as scoring assessments and entering data in our database. Often these activities were a joint effort because not everyone could easily translate Boston accents or knew who the children's book character Inspector Gadget was. Although we cannot name all of these assistants here, we want to thank each and every one of them for their contributions. All of their hard work on these transcripts has now paid off doubly in that the transcripts have been made available for further analysis by other researchers through an Internet database called the Child Language Data Exchange System (http://childes.psy.cmu.edu/data/local.html).

Organizing data collection at the children's schools became evermore complicated as children moved from a relatively small number of preschools into a large group of elementary schools, then into far-flung middle and high schools. Consequently, the research team had to negotiate entry into an increasing number of schools each year to collect data on the students' language and literacy abilities, and, in middle and high school, to interview teachers and guidance counselors as well as the students themselves. Both Stephanie Ross Harris and Petra Nicholson were invaluable in these efforts. Our well-worn collection of maps of the cities and towns of eastern Massachusetts, acquired before the advent of Internet mapping sites such as Mapquest, attest to this effort.

Processing and analyzing the data from the study involved an outstanding group of graduate students. Joy Amulya, Diane Beals, Jeanne De Temple, Brenda Kurland, Kevin Roach, and Miriam Smith, along with Michelle V. Porche, were instrumental in this aspect of the study. Claudia Cooper, Jane Katz, and Zehava Weizman also made good use of the data from the study. More recent work on this book was supported by the efforts of Young-Suk Kim and Harriet Tenenbaum. Compensations were few, but appreciated. Presentations at academic conferences made it possible to experience in-suite pizza in Chicago and feather boas in New Orleans, as well as the opportunity to push the team to finish analyses, interpret findings, and present those findings to interested colleagues.

Somehow, it all happened. Presentations were made; reports and proposals were written; articles were sent off for review, revised, and published. Theses were written and doctorates were awarded. A book on the preschool aspects of the study, *Beginning Literacy with Language: Young Children Learning at Home and School,* edited by David K. Dickinson and Patton O. Tabors, was completed and published by Paul H. Brookes Publishing Co. in 2001. And now, finally, we have a book that wraps up the longitudinal findings of the study, and that highlights the particular challenges facing even good readers as they enter adolescence and larger, less student-centered schools. Our hope is that it will contribute to the discussion about improving education in the United States for all children throughout the schooling years.

The Home–School Study of Language and Literacy Development would not have been possible without the involvement of a very generous group of families. They gave us permission, year after year, to come into their homes and their children's schools and shared their lives with us. Knowing that they themselves would not benefit directly from the research, the parents and children participated with the knowledge that their contribution would improve education for others. We are extremely grateful to them, and it is to them that we dedicate this book.

1

The Ever-Narrowing Path to School Success

Two parallel conversations about education are going on in the United States. One of them celebrates improvements in primary reading instruction, pointing to both rising scores and shrinking racial achievement gaps for students in the early grades. For example, an impressive increase in fourth-grade National Assessment of Educational Progress (NAEP) reading scores occurred between 1971 and 2004,[1] and during the same period, the gap in performance attributable to race or to social class lessened (although it did not disappear), suggesting that educators are doing a better job of teaching reading in all schools. The other conversation is more despairing. It centers on alarming school dropout rates; poor performance by American middle- and high-school students in international comparisons of reading, math, and science skills; and the underpreparation of high school graduates for participation in the knowledge economy, in which the production of ideas and communication have overtaken manufacturing. How can this be? If schools are succeeding at teaching students to read by fourth grade, why not expect equivalent levels of success in the later grades? Should good fourth-grade readers not find it easy to read in the later grades, and to learn the math, social studies, and science to which literacy skills contribute?

In this book, we focus precisely on this paradox by describing what happened to a group of children from low-income families as they proceeded from preschool through middle and high school. When we started the Home–School Study of Language and Literacy Development, we were interested primarily in how the children's literacy skills developed. But in the process of following these students—many of whom were excellent readers in fourth grade—through adolescence and beyond, we were confronted with the many factors besides literacy

---

[1]Results from the long-term NAEP assessment studies are available at http://nces.ed.gov/nationsreportcard/ltt (retrieved August 1, 2006).

skills that influenced the children's experiences in school and their ultimate success or failure as students.

One way to represent what we saw is as a series of jigsaw puzzles of increasing complexity (see Figure 1.1). A kindergartner has a fairly simple puzzle to put together in order to do well in school. This puzzle is made of large pieces consisting mostly of appropriate attentiveness and oral language skills. In the primary grades, the puzzle expands to include more pieces, and smaller pieces with more complicated interlockings. But this is still a simple puzzle compared with the later grades. If a child is having a problem in first or second grade, the range of possible solutions a literacy expert might suggest to the teacher is quite small (e.g., try some supplementary instruction in phonological awareness, check the child's fluency in letter recognition and mapping letters to the sounds they stand for, try reteaching basic word-reading skills, be sure the child can read high-frequency words that are irregularly spelled, provide lots of practice to develop automaticity). Of course, the fact that there is only a small number of puzzle pieces in the early grades places a huge premium on the skills that are required; children with dyslexia or children who have not been taught to read effectively are in a perilous situation because success in first grade is pretty much all about reading—indeed—about reading fairly simple and familiar texts.

By the middle grades, however, the prescription for students who are struggling with reading is much more complicated because success in reading is dependent not only on possessing word-reading skills but also on knowing vocabulary, being able to process longer and more complicated texts, having the background knowledge presupposed by the text and the curriculum, and having some reasonable level of interest in the text and motivation to persist in reading it. The many pieces that make up the adolescent literacy puzzle represent far more varied domains than just the skills of word reading. Thus, the prescription for helping the older struggling reader is not so straightforward as for the younger struggling reader. It might involve reteaching word-reading skills somehow missed in the first and second grades, or perhaps teaching the student to read those words automatically or to apply those word-reading skills to multisyllabic words. Or, perhaps it would require helping the student to increase his or her vocabulary and greatly extending his or her background knowledge. Perhaps it would mean finding reading materials of greater interest to the older struggling reader than many sixth-grade geography texts or seventh-grade English literature selections tend to be, and/or identifying procedures to get the student interested in the material being taught. Perhaps it would require helping the student see that reading with comprehension requires work and gets better if practiced. Perhaps it would require even more far-reaching interventions in the student's motivational system, for instance, by showing the student the relationship between school success and his or her own long-term goals, or by helping the student to resolve the familial or interpersonal problems that interfere with the focus on learning.

The story we tell in this book is the story of how much more complicated predicting and supporting academic success is for adolescents than for primary

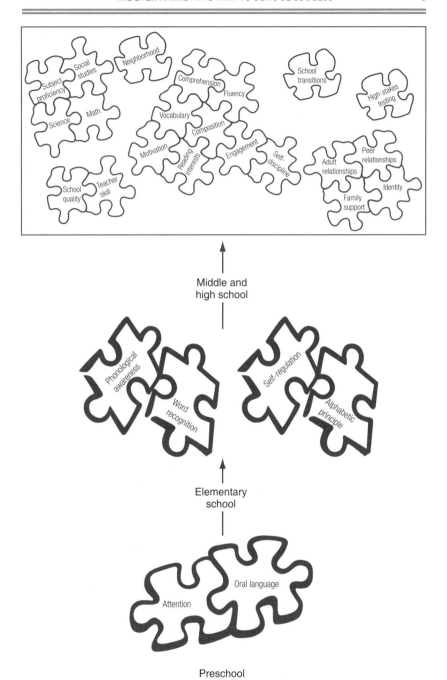

Figure 1.1. The increasingly complex puzzle of academic success. As a child moves from pre-school to middle school to high school, more and more literacy pieces must come together in order for the student to achieve success in literacy.

grade students. We show that academic success in the earliest grades is largely a product of children's language and literacy skills, whereas academic success in the later grades is likely only if many factors converge. Students need good basic literacy skills, but they also need familiarity with the academic language of the texts, access to the knowledge presupposed by the texts and the curriculum, motivation to succeed joined with an understanding of what it takes, reasonably positive social relationships with fellow students and teachers, and freedom from serious disruptions in their familial or personal lives. In other words, many things have to go right to ensure academic success for adolescents, and only a few need to go wrong to imperil academic outcomes.

Of course, most adolescents do encounter some problems at school or at home, and we do not mean to suggest that every setback leads directly to school failure or dropout. But we will show, by analyzing the school histories of a group of children growing up in low-income families, the kinds of vulnerabilities to which such students are subject and the ways in which events outside of their control can undermine the school performance even of students with adequate academic skills.

FOCUSING ON LITERACY

The typical 5-year-old student arrives at school eager to meet the teacher, to join in activities with classmates, and, most important, to learn to read. Reading is the cornerstone skill in the eyes of primary grade teachers and indeed, of their students. Children who settle down to learning letters and sounds in kindergarten, much evidence suggests, go on to success in learning to read words and short texts in first grade; in reading and comprehending longer and more complex texts in the later elementary grades; and in learning math, history, and science in large part through reading about them. These children succeed in the high-stakes tests required for promotion and graduation and ultimately, in further education and employment. Such children are the "norm"—those who arrive at school with the expected skills and who make the expected progress from year to year.

Not all children follow this trajectory, however. A striking and depressing fact about school outcomes in the United States is the persistence of differences in school success among socioeconomic groups, as measured by reading outcomes in the primary grades, by retention rates, by school dropout rates, and by failure to qualify for entry to or graduation from institutions of higher education (McLoyd, 1998). Explanations for these differences range from the sociological to the cultural to the psychological. A frequently offered hypothesis, and one that seems to underpin federal policies in the early 21st century, is that such differences simply reflect teachers' low expectations (Wigfield & Harold, 1992) and misguided instructional practices in the early grades. The argument supporting these policies rests on two, not always explicit, prior assumptions: first, that schools, if provided with sufficient motivation and adequate guidance from research about effective reading instruction, can teach all children to the same high level; and second, that successful literacy acquisition in the primary grades will lead inexorably to success in the challenges of comprehending and reading for learning in the middle and secondary grades. Both of these assumptions can be challenged.

Rothstein (2004) countered the first assumption by arguing that social class differences in achievement reflect a wide array of differences in the circumstances of children's lives, all of which lead to differential capacity to take advantage of school. In his works, he cites large social class differences in children's access to the kinds of preschool and after-school care settings that predict academic performance, in their access to literacy and language experiences at home, and in aspects of their health that might influence their attendance at school and their capacity for sustained classroom learning (e.g., asthma, ear infections, poor vision, poor nutrition). Rothstein argues that it is unrealistic to think that even excellent schools could entirely compensate for the many extra challenges that children from low-income families face.

The second assumption—that good early literacy skills lead automatically to success with later literacy—is also questionable in light of considerable counterevidence. Of course, its converse, that poor early literacy outcomes increase a student's risk of failure in later grades, is widely accepted. Stanovich's (1986) formulation of this scenario, which he called the *Matthew effect* (referring to the Bible verse from the book of Matthew [XXV:29, KJV], about the rich getting richer and the poor getting poorer), is this: A child enters kindergarten or first grade lacking skills that teachers and literacy curricula presuppose. The child is confused, frustrated, or simply unaffected by the literacy instruction provided. The teacher, whether because of inadequate preparation, insufficient support, inadequate time, or the constraints of prescribed curricula, cannot individualize his or her instruction to meet the child's needs. Thus, the student never masters the basics of reading in the primary grades, comes to dislike and avoid reading, and, therefore, fails to engage in reading the simple texts that would build accuracy and fluency. Nonfluent readers read slowly and with effort, which makes them unlikely to read very much. Because it is through reading that comprehension skills, vocabulary, and world knowledge grow, such a child ends up falling behind classmates in a wide array of skills, although the initial problem may simply have been a small and perhaps fully remediable developmental lag in kindergarten or first grade.

Research by Stanovich and his colleagues amply documents the predictive relationship of wide reading to vocabulary and world knowledge (Stanovich, West, Cunningham, Cipielewski, & Siddiqui, 1996; Stanovich, West, & Harrison, 1995), and that early success in reading predicts later reading outcomes (Cunningham & Stanovich, 1997; Echols, West, Stanovich, & Zehr, 1996). So, there is evidence supporting the claim of continuity between early and later literacy success and, in particular, continuity between early and later failure. But there is also considerable evidence suggesting that an early successful start with literacy is not enough to ensure later literacy success for all children.

Of course, accuracy and fluency in word reading are prerequisite to comprehension, but they are hardly sufficient to ensure it. Many students who read the relatively simple texts of the primary grades with ease encounter difficulties with the dense, syntactically complex, information-rich, vocabulary-laden texts with multiple interpretations that they are expected to read in the higher grades (RAND Reading Study Group, 2002). Even those who can read the words in the more complex texts accurately may not be able to construct new or to elaborate on old knowledge schemas reliably on the basis of written texts. The question remains why some learners make the transition from reading simple to more complex texts easily, whereas others encounter problems.

Evidence from NAEP indicates that an alarmingly high proportion of 13- and 17-year-olds in U.S. schools perform in the "below basic" category in reading—meaning that they are unable to identify the main idea in an age-appropriate passage, let alone to elaborate on an idea encountered through reading. Furthermore, while cross-age comparisons suggest that U.S. students on average show continued growth in reading skills across the school years, they improve more between 9 and 13 years of age than between 13 and 17 years of age (National Center for Education Statistics, 2005). This pattern suggests that some attention is paid to comprehension instruction in the middle grades, but that secondary instruction fails to acknowledge how much high school students still have to learn about deep comprehension.

Comparisons of U.S. students with those in other developed countries also counter the assumption that good early performance in reading leads automatically to success. The Program for International Student Assessment (PISA) of 15-Year-Olds (Lemke et al., 2001; Topping, Valtin, Roller, Brozo, & Dionisio, 2003) indicates that U.S. students perform quite well in comparison with those in other developed countries in the early grades but sink in the rankings as older students are tested. PISA analyses showed that 15-year-olds in the United States read less well than do 15-year-olds in a dozen other countries, including some that spend considerably less per pupil on education than does the United States (for instance, Korea spends less than half per pupil annually, and the United Kingdom spends about one third less, yet students in both countries far outperform U.S. counterparts on standardized literacy assessments; see OECD, 2001). Such indications from performance data have generated growing concerns in the practice and policy community about adolescent literacy.[2] Many U.S. schools are evidently

---

[2]Recent policy-oriented initiatives that focus on adolescent literacy include the Carnegie Corporation's Advisory Council on Advancing Adolescent Literacy, the NICHD program of grants focused on adolescent literacy, efforts of the Alliance for Excellent Education and the National Governors Association, and the production by the Carnegie Corporation of New York of reports such as: *Reading Next: A Vision for Action and Research in Middle and High School Literacy* (Biancarosa & Snow, 2005).

failing in their ongoing support of literacy development, especially given considerable expenditures on education. PISA analyses also showed some evidence for a positive association between socioeconomic status of the family and student achievement. However, whereas some countries provide counterevidence that public education can level the playing field, U.S. schools that serve low-income students and students from ethnic minority communities are much more likely to be in the bottom quartile in reading proficiency (OECD, 2001).

FOCUSING ON ACADEMIC ACHIEVEMENT

Much evidence indicates that schools are not doing a great job of teaching students to read after fourth grade. But as noted previously, even if we were solving the literacy challenge for middle and secondary school students, that would not necessarily solve the larger problems that are often entwined with literacy in public discussion. We will present data suggesting that many students, even some with excellent literacy skills, become unmotivated and disaffected in the middle grades. Although their performance on the literacy assessments we administered continued to be good, their performance on the tasks assigned by their teachers was far from adequate. Some of these students were struggling with the new academic challenges they faced, in some cases with inadequate personal attention from any adults at home or at school. Some students were fully capable of meeting the academic challenges but had decided not to bother. Some were often absent from school because of conflicts with other students or because of distractions associated with family conflicts. Many were rudderless in large and rather impersonal high schools, unable either to connect what was going on in their classes to their own goals or to connect with any adults who could offer them guidance and support.

However, many of the students we followed were academically successful as adolescents, graduating from high school and going on to further education or to satisfying jobs. Some of these academically successful students were among the high scorers on our literacy assessments, but surprisingly, some of them looked only average or weak on our tests. In other words, their literacy skills were not irrelevant to their academic achievement, but neither were their skills sufficient to explain it. What differentiated the students who met our criterion for academic success, graduating from high school more or less on time or getting a GED, from those who did not? To answer this question, we explored a wide array of information we had available: the students' responses in interviews and on evaluations of their motivation and orientation to learning; their writings about their own futures; their parents' and their teachers' views of them; their grades and other information from their school records; and the kinds of schools and school programs they attended. The answer that emerged from this exploration was richly textured, suggesting that students can take several possible paths to success but also that they face a very large number of stumbling blocks along the way.

Perhaps the most widely advocated, and certainly the most expensive, current policy response to the challenges of adolescent literacy is the establishment of small high schools, in which students have a higher likelihood of personal connection with adults. The Gates Foundation invested more than $50 million in 2006 alone toward the establishment of such schools, although direct evidence that such schools help is not yet available. The results we present suggest that, indeed, students who had more personal connections with adults in their schools did better academically—but we also found that there were many avenues for establishing such connections even within large schools. Furthermore, other aspects of students' lives were also important in predicting their likelihood of success.

We hope, then, that the results of this study will contribute information to the urgent, ongoing national conversation about promoting student learning in the middle and high schools serving low-income students. In our small sample, 26% of the students dropped out before completing high school, and one of those who did complete high school coursework did not receive a diploma because he was unable to pass the state-mandated achievement test. In the country as a whole, estimated overall dropout rates range from 25% to 40% in different studies, and as high as 50% for African American and Latino males in group-level analyses (see Orfield, 2004, for an extended discussion of dropout rates). Even if we accept the most conservative estimates of dropout rates, the picture is alarming, because without a high school diploma, an individual's access to jobs that would support a family or offer a reasonable level of career advancement is very unlikely (Murnane & Levy, 1996). Our findings suggest that improving academic success, like improving literacy outcomes, is entirely possible, but it will require a multifaceted approach that takes into account the full array of obstacles students face along the way.

2

Closing the Literacy Achievement Gap and Promoting Reading for Learning

Two Challenges

In this book, we report analyses of the literacy and academic development of a group of children from low-income families. This study was originally undertaken to answer questions about the experiences during the preschool years that promoted success in reading in Grades 1–4. In particular, the goal was to evaluate the relative contributions of early experiences leading to good code-related skills (e.g., letter recognition, phonological awareness) versus those leading to rich language skills (e.g., vocabulary, listening comprehension, production of narratives and definitions) to fourth-grade reading outcomes. As in many longitudinal studies, the temptation to continue following the participants was irresistible, so we continued collecting data beyond Grade 4 and in areas that transcended our original focus on literacy.

The data we present here enable us to assess the degree to which early success in literacy does indeed predict later literacy and school achievement. More specifically, though, the data enable us to ask questions about 1) precisely what aspects of early literacy achievement predict robustly to later achievement, 2) what aspects of later achievement relate most strongly to early literacy success, and 3) what child characteristics and environmental factors influence those predictive relationships.

The subsequent chapters in this book report analyses of the achievement of the students we followed from kindergarten through high school. We have previously published an extensive analysis of the experiences in home and preschool classrooms that predicted these children's kindergarten literacy and language skills (Dickinson & Tabors, 2001); those findings are summarized in the following section as background to the new analyses. As will be documented in later chapters, considerable continuity can be found for this group of learners from kindergarten outcomes to later literacy outcomes. However, factors other than early literacy skills also have a great impact on where these students end up academically. In other words, although the Matthew effect (see Chapter 1) largely holds for this group, its effect is limited to literacy. Academic success or failure depends on more than just literacy skills, and thus, explaining it requires a much more complicated story.

CHILDREN FROM LOW-INCOME HOMES

The students reported on in this book have participated in a longitudinal study (referred to as the Home–School Study) that began in 1988 in the metropolitan Boston area when members of the first group were 3 years old. (A second group was added the following year, bringing the number of children in the study to 83.) The group consisted of children from low-income homes where English was the primary language.

Our major goal in first conceptualizing this work was to identify the experiences that led to the development of academic oral language skills during the preschool years. Our previous work with school-age children (e.g., Davidson, Kline, & Snow, 1986; Dickinson & Snow, 1987; Snow, 1990; Velasco, 1989) had suggested that good readers were distinguished by better control over certain kinds of oral discourse—what we now call *academic language* (previously referred to as *decontextualized language* or *extended discourse*). Oral discourse skills such as telling coherent stories, making convincing arguments, or providing succinct and communicatively effective definitions of words were correlated with literacy success in the middle grades. And this is not surprising, because the texts that middle-grade students need to comprehend are full of linguistic complexities characteristic of coherent stories, arguments, and definitions. Furthermore, our early work suggested that social class differences in these oral language skills were present at kindergarten (DeTemple, 2001; Snow & Dickinson, 1990, 1991); thus, such skills might well be implicated in explaining the poor literacy outcomes of children from low-income homes. At a time when literacy researchers were quite single-mindedly focused on phonological awareness and letter knowledge as predictors of literacy success and word reading as the major literacy outcome worthy of assessment, we felt it important to redress the balance by seeking evidence about the role of language skills and the predictors of reading comprehension.

A basic presumption of our work was that conversational and academic language stemmed from two different developmental origins (see Figure 2.1). We

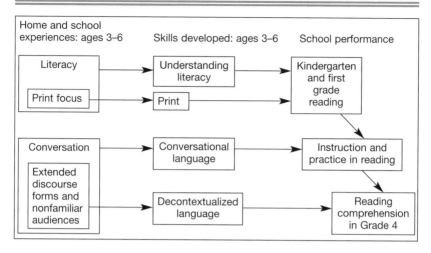

Figure 2.1. Model of relations between language and literacy development. (Reprinted by permission of Catherine E. Snow and the Association for Childhood Education International, 17904 Georgia Avenue, Suite 215, Olney, MD. Copyright © 1991 by the Association.)

hoped to identify the precursors of academic language skill in familial and preschool interactions and to confirm the relationship of early academic language skill to later reading accomplishments. We assumed, along with most of our colleagues, that these oral language skills would relate to reading only in Grade 3 or later, after children had accomplished the task of learning how to decode. Thus, our original plan was to carry out a prospective longitudinal study through Grade 4.

We chose to limit our participants to individuals from low-income families for a number of reasons: 1) we wanted to ensure a wide range of literacy outcomes, including sufficient numbers of children likely to have difficulties learning to read; 2) we did not want to spend our limited resources on replicating previous studies that had described interaction in middle-income families; and 3) we were less interested in a comparison of middle-income with working-class families than in a description of variation within a lower-income group.

CHARACTERISTICS OF THE HOME–SCHOOL STUDY PARTICIPANTS

Demographic information about the families whose children have participated in the Home–School Study was collected at the first home visit when the children were 3 years old. Table 2.1 displays the demographic characteristics culled from these interviews for the original participants and for the subsequent constellations of the group, reflecting attrition over the years.

Table 2.1. Sample demographic characteristics for five data collection periods using variables from the original home visit (child age 3 years old) to determine potential effects of attrition

	Original (n = 83)	Kindergarten (n = 74)	4th grade (n = 59)	7th grade (n = 54)	10th grade (n = 41)
Gender					
Girls	51%	51%	53%[a]	59%	61%
Boys	49%	49%	48%	41%	39%
Race/ethnicity					
African descent (African American, Caribbean)	23%	22%[a]	20%	20%	22%
White	64%	64%	66%	67%	66%
Latino	7%	8%	7%	6%	2%
Mixed race	6%	7%	7%	7%	10%
Maternal education level at start of study					
No diploma	21%	22%	20%	22%[a]	20%[a]
GED	17%	17%	22%	23%	22%
High school graduate	62%	61%	58%	56%	59%
Annual family income at start of study					
Less than $10,000	46%	43%	41%	41%[a]	34%[a]
$10,000–$15,000	11%	12%	10%	11%	10%
$15,000–$20,000	17%	18%	20%	20%	24%
$20,000–$25,000	10%	11%	9%	7%	7%
More than $25,000	16%	16%	20%	20%	24%
Primary income source at start of study					
Primary caregiver	21%[a]	22%[a]	24%[a]	24%	27%
Spouse/partner	33%	34%	34%	35%	39%
AFDC/welfare	45%	42%	41%	39%	32%
Child support	2%	3%	2%	2%	2%
Language assessment of child					
Mean MLU (SD)	2.96 (0.66)	2.97 (0.66)	3.01 (0.67)	3.03 (0.67)	3.03 (0.68)
range (3-year-old toy play)	(1.17–4.22) (n = 75)	(1.17–4.22) (n = 74)	(1.17–4.22) (n = 59)	(1.17–4.22) (n = 54)	(1.17–4.22) (n = 41)

Note: No significant difference was found for any of the demographic or language assessment variables between any of the given time periods.

[a]Numbers may not add up to 100% because of rounding.

Key: MLU, mean length of utterance.

At the beginning of the study, we had an equal number of boys and girls. Sixty-four percent of the children in the group were White,[1] whereas the rest were of African descent (African American and Caribbean: 23%), Latino (7%), or mixed (6%) origins. Sixty-two percent of the mothers had graduated from high school, and an additional 17% had earned a General Equivalency Diploma (GED). Twenty-one percent of the mothers, however, had not attained a high school degree.

At the beginning of the study, approximately half (46%) of the households had an annual family income of less than $10,000. In most cases, these were the same parents (45%) whose main source of income came from Aid to Families with Dependent Children (AFDC; now called Temporary Assistance for Needy Families, or TANF). The remaining families reported annual incomes ranging from more than $10,000 to more than $25,000. In 21% of the families, the primary caregiver (the mother) was the primary source of income, and in 33% of the families, the mother's spouse or partner was the main source of income.

The children's mean length of utterance (MLU), indicating the complexity of their sentences when interacting with their mothers during a toy play session, averaged 2.96 (SD 0.66). The average age of the children at the first home visit was 46 months, placing the MLU of this group below the predicted range (3.21–4.97) at this age (Miller, 1981).

As shown in Table 2.1, there has been attrition from the group over the course of the longitudinal project, but the attrition has been unbiased, and the demographic characteristics of the group available for long-term longitudinal analysis remain much the same as those of the original group.

PRESCHOOL FINDINGS

Home visits were made to the children who were participating in the Home–School Study when they were 3, 4, and 5 years old, and classroom visits were made to the children who were in preschool classrooms at 3 years old and to all children at 4 years old. The purpose of these visits was to collect data about the language and literacy environments to which the children were being exposed. Findings from this data collection period, reported in the volume edited by Dickinson and Tabors (2001), are summarized briefly here to provide background information.

Home Language and Literacy Environment

Home visits were scheduled for three intervals (when the children were 3, 4, and 5 years old) so that we could observe and audiotape each mother and her child in

---

[1]The term *White* is used rather than *Caucasian* throughout this book to reflect terminology commonly used by the U.S. Bureau of the Census and researchers.

a variety of activities. These activities included reading books and playing with a standard set of toys with the 3- and 4-year-olds and adding playing with a set of magnets when the children were 5 years old. In addition, an audiotape recorder was left with the mother to tape a family mealtime, which, like the other interactions, was subsequently transcribed and analyzed. Also, mothers were interviewed on topics related to family circumstances and literacy practices.

After transcription and verification of the audiotapes, the mother–child interactions were coded for various types of extended discourse, including nonimmediate talk (DeTemple, 2001), fantasy talk (Katz, 2001), explanatory and narrative talk (Beals, 2001), and science process talk (Tabors, Roach, & Snow, 2001), as well as for the presence of rare words—words that would be unusual to find in the vocabulary of young children (Tabors, Beals, & Weizman, 2001). The mothers' interviews were coded for demographic information (as seen in Table 2.1), as well as family literacy practices (DeTemple, 2001).

In order to reduce the number of variables for further analysis, three composites were constructed (Tabors, Roach & Snow, 2001; see Figure 2.2). The first composite, Maternal Extended Discourse, consists of the sum of the proportion of each of the following types of discourse in each mother's interactions with her child: nonimmediate talk during book reading, fantasy talk during toy play, explanatory and narrative talk during mealtime, and science process talk during

Child's age in years			Home visit data sources	Variables	Composite
3	4	5			
x	x	x	Book reading	Mothers' percentage of nonimmediate talk	Maternal Extended Discourse
x	x	x	Toy play	Mothers' percentage of fantasy talk	
x	x	x	Mealtime	Mothers' percentage of explanatory talk	
				Mothers' percentage of narrative talk	
		x	Magnet play	Mothers' percentage of science process talk	
x	x	x	Toy play	Mothers' rare word density	Rare Word Density
x	x	x	Mealtime	Mothers' rare word density	
x	x		Maternal interview	Mothers' reported home support for literacy	Home Support for Literacy

Figure 2.2. Developing the Home Language and Literacy Environment composites from home-visit data (for children at ages 3, 4, and 5).

magnet play. The second composite, Rare Word Density, consists of the sum of the proportion of rare words in the mothers' interactions during toy play and mealtimes. The third composite, Home Support for Literacy, summarizes answers from the first two interviews concerning frequency and variety of literacy practices in the home.

Preschool Language and Literacy Environment

During the preschool visits, teachers were audiotaped during group times, free play periods, and mealtimes, and they were videotaped during large-group book reading. The child participant was also audiorecorded during an extended free play period. Researchers observed the classroom curriculum and administered teacher questionnaires.

Teacher talk from the audio and video recordings was transcribed, verified, and coded (Cote, 2001; Smith, 2001). Child talk was coded directly from the audiotapes, and classroom observations and teacher questionnaires were also coded (Dickinson, 2001a, 2001b, 2001c). Only variables from the 4-year-old classroom visit were used in further analyses, as many of the children were not yet in classroom settings at age 3.

As shown in Figure 2.3, a selected group of variables were combined into composites representing Teacher Extended Discourse, Classroom Exposure to Rare Words, and Classroom Curriculum (Dickinson, 2001c).

Preschool visit data sources	Variables	Composite
Group time	Teachers' group focusing talk Teachers' cognitive extending talk	Teacher Extended Discourse
Book reading	Teachers' percentage of book analysis talk	
Free play	Teachers' percentage of extending talk	
Mealtimes	Teachers' percentage of rare words	Classroom Exposure to Rare Words
Group time	Teachers' percentage of rare words	
Free play	Teachers' percentage of rare words Children's rare word types	
Curriculum observations	Quality of writing program Curriculum content	Classroom Curriculum
Teacher interview	Pedagogical belief: need to promote social and emotional development (negative)	

Figure 2.3. Developing the Preschool Language and Literacy Environment composites from preschool visit data (for children at age 4).

Predicting Kindergarten Language and Literacy Skills from Home and Preschool Environments

When the children in the study were in kindergarten, we administered a battery of language and literacy tests that included an original, researcher-developed narrative production task (the Bear Story), an emergent literacy test (Mason & Stewart, 1989), and the Peabody Picture Vocabulary Test–Revised (PPVT-R; Dunn & Dunn, 1981; see Snow, Tabors, & Dickinson, 2001, pp. 10–12 for further description of these tests). The narrative production task was scored for both length of production and presence of story elements combined in a total score. The emergent literacy test involved subtests for writing concepts, letter recognition, story and print concepts, sounds in words, and environmental print, again combined in a total score. The normed score equivalent from the PPVT-R was used to indicate receptive vocabulary ability.

Regression analyses were performed to determine what aspects of the home and preschool environments could predict kindergarten outcomes on these three measures. The results of these regression analyses are presented in Table 2.2 as final models predicting narrative production, emergent literacy, and receptive vocabulary. These results, which are discussed at length in Tabors, Snow, and Dickinson (2001), led to the following conclusions:

- Vocabulary development was most powerfully predicted by exposure to rare words in the home and exposure to rare words and teacher extended discourse in the preschool classroom.

- No single home or preschool variable stood out as most powerful in predicting narrative development, although narrative skill was significantly associated with exposure to extended discourse and literacy experiences in the home and with teacher extended discourse and the presence of a curriculum in the preschool classroom.

- Emergent literacy skills were best predicted by rare word density at home and by teacher extended discourse at preschool.

- Both home and preschool variables were significantly related to all three outcomes, and both continued to make independent contributions when entered into the same regression model.

- It was possible to explain more of the variance in outcomes for vocabulary and emergent literacy than for narrative skill, the developmental antecedents of which remain more obscure in these data.

CONTINUITY IN LITERACY DEVELOPMENT

The work from the first 3 years of the Home–School Study pointed to the value of high-quality environments during the preschool years in preparing children for

Table 2.2. Final models predicting narrative production, emergent literacy, and receptive vocabulary in kindergarten

Model	Home environment composites			Preschool environment composites			
	Rare Word Density	Maternal Extended Discourse	Home Support for Literacy	Teacher Extended Discourse	Classroom Curriculum	Classroom Exposure to Rare Words	R^2
	β ($SE\ \beta$)	β ($SE\ \beta$)	β ($SE\ \beta$)	β ($SE\ \beta$)	β ($SE\ \beta$)	β ($SE\ \beta$)	
Narrative production	−0.01 (.01)	0.009 (.007)	0.06 (.09)	0.29 (.38)	0.52 (.34)	0.38 (.33)	.33*
Emergent literacy	0.02 (.02)	0.00 (.007)	0.11 (.11)	1.29** (.44)	0.38 (.39)	0.65~ (.39)	.52***
Receptive vocabulary	0.13* (.06)	0.007 (.03)	0.71~ (.40)	3.58* (1.67)	2.42 (1.49)	1.83 (1.47)	.56***

Note: Child's gender, child's race, child's mean length of utterance at age 3, mother's education, and reported family income are included in these analyses as control variables.

Source: Tabors, Snow, & Dickinson (2001).

~$p < .10$; *$p < .05$; **$p < .01$; ***$p < .001$

literacy learning. Indeed, this conclusion from our study supports the emphasis within current federal education policy on funding to improve preschool and primary literacy instruction through such mechanisms as the No Child Left Behind (NCLB) Act of 2001 (PL107-110), which also included Reading First and Early Reading First. This policy reflects the robust finding that children who enter school with well-developed early literacy skills will likely learn to read without undue difficulty in the primary grades and be successful readers in later grades. Conversely, children who enter kindergarten with poor emergent literacy skills are likely to encounter difficulties learning to read in first and second grade and to remain struggling readers throughout their school years.

A major question has been to what degree the persistent, long-term difficulties experienced by children who are slow starters in reading reflect those children's inherent and difficult-to-remediate learning problems, or whether the mere fact of starting behind launches a cascade of learning challenges that most children are unable to overcome, as suggested by the Matthew effect hypothesis (Stanovich, 1986). Children from middle-income families and children attending suburban schools are much less likely to experience the fully articulated version of the Matthew effect for reading because they are less subject to each of the unfortunate events in the sequence. Children whose parents have more economic and educational resources are likely to arrive at school with the skills that primary teachers and reading curricula presuppose. Children in suburban schools are less likely than those in urban schools to experience poor reading instruction in the early grades. Parents with economic and educational resources are likely to intervene quickly by offering help with homework, securing the service of tutors, or requesting extra attention from the teacher if their children start to struggle with reading. And, if the quick intervention is insufficient, such parents can use their resources to seek more drastic solutions (e.g., moving to a better school district, securing admission to a private school). Children from low-income families and children from urban areas are both more likely to encounter poor schooling and are more vulnerable to its effects, and their families often lack the knowledge and the social capital to organize interruptions to the accumulation of reading challenges (Lareau & Horvat, 1999; Monkman, Ronald, & Theramene, 2005; Toutkoushian & Curtis, 2005).

Considerable research evidence (see Snow, Burns, & Griffin, 1998, for a review) has converged on the conclusion that many of the children who experience reading problems in the middle grades could have avoided those problems with excellent primary reading instruction. In other words, the overwhelming weight of the evidence suggests a high level of continuity from early to later performance within the domain of literacy. Nonetheless, as noted previously, children who are successful in primary-grade reading may well encounter difficulties with the new reading tasks of the middle and secondary grades. In this book, we take the hypothesis of continuity as our starting point, exploring its applicability in explaining the academic achievement of low-income children from the age of 3 through secondary school.

One reason to focus so heavily on literacy development is that literacy is the gatekeeper skill for academic success. Children who cannot read well are denied access to most of the learning activities that occur in the later grades. In this book, we present longitudinal data on the literacy development of low-income children with two purposes: 1) to document over a longer time-span than previously studied the continuities and discontinuities in literacy development, and 2) to pursue questions about the relation of literacy to other indicators of academic success, including grades, on-time promotion, teacher ratings, motivation, and avoidance of behavioral problems. In the process, we hope to contribute to a deeper understanding of the determinants of both literacy outcomes and of low-income adolescents' success in school.

Analyzing the Nature of Continuity in Literacy Performance

What are we looking for as we evaluate the existence of continuities in literacy development? First, it is clear that we are talking about heterotypic continuity; 5-year-olds are not, after all, in most cases actually reading, so the continuity hypothesis reflects the prediction of *real reading abilities* from early reading *related* skills. Five-year-olds' *emergent literacy capacities*—the ability to recognize letters, to identify and segment phonemes, to produce invented spellings, to understand some basic concepts about print, and to understand the uses and functions of literacy—relate to their later ability to read words and texts (Hoff-Ginsberg & Tardif, 1995; Purcell-Gates, 1996). In addition, 5-year-olds' oral language abilities—specifically vocabulary size and the ability to tell stories and give definitions—also predict their later reading skill. How do we understand these relationships? Do all of these predictors relate equally strongly to reading outcomes? Can one or another of them be demonstrated to have a central or causal relationship to reading outcomes? And, do they all relate to the same aspects of reading outcomes, or are there differential relationships to different aspects of reading skill?

Answering these questions is made more difficult by the fact of moderate to high intercorrelations among all of these various predictors. Child-ren growing up in homes or attending preschools that support oral language development also tend to have many opportunities to engage in book reading, to observe parents' literacy, and in other ways to develop strong emergent literacy skills (Denton & West, 2002; Rathbun & West, 2004; West, Denton, & Reaney, 2000).

Although one might expect that emergent literacy skills would relate most strongly to early word-reading outcomes, and that vocabulary and other language skills might show relationships only to later emerging comprehension; in fact, previous findings with the group we focus on and other studies make clear that oral language skills relate to the earliest reading outcomes (Cunningham, Perry,

& Stanovich, 2001; Snow, Tabors, Nicholson, & Kurland, 1995) and that print
and phonemic awareness skills continue to correlate with reading scores into the
middle elementary years (Freebody & Anderson, 1983).

THE DETERMINACY OF VOCABULARY

Perhaps the most robust finding in the field of literacy is the high correlation
between vocabulary and reading comprehension (Anderson & Freebody, 1981;
Hart & Risley, 1995; Stahl, 2003). Vocabulary scores of 5-year-olds predict reading outcomes as early as first grade (e.g., Snow et al., 1995) and continue to predict reading outcomes through the elementary years. This correlation serves as
evidence for a variety of hypotheses—as evidence that comprehension depends on
access to the meaning of words encountered in print, as evidence that wide reading with comprehension generates vocabulary knowledge, as evidence that homes
and schools that promote high-level reading skills tend also to promote other skills
related to comprehension, and as another consequence of the Matthew effect.

Common to the various hypotheses explaining the vocabulary-
comprehension nexus, though, is the presupposition that this relation is to be
expected. Looking at any sixth-grade social studies text, any high school biology
text, or at the front page of the *New York Times* makes clear that comprehending
such texts depends on knowing the meanings of fairly infrequently occurring
words, such as *negotiate, govern, evolve, respire, conspiracy, pollution, allegation,
catastrophe, fraud,* and *deficit.* Anticipating the findings that will be presented in
more technical detail in Chapter 3, we present in Table 2.3 correlations between
kindergarten vocabulary and later reading-comprehension scores from the students in our longitudinal study. These positive correlations are difficult to explain

Table 2.3. Correlations between receptive vocabulary in kindergarten and listening and
reading comprehension in kindergarten through 10th grade

Grade	Receptive vocabulary[a] in kindergarten	Listening and reading comprehension measures	(N)
K	.59***	Listening comprehension[b]	(74)
1st	.45***	Word recognition[c]	(64)
4th	.56***	Word recognition[c]	(57)
4th	.62***	Reading comprehension[d]	(56)
7th	.69***	Reading comprehension[d]	(54)
10th	.60***	Reading comprehension[d]	(41)

[a]Standard score, Peabody Picture Vocabulary Test–Revised (Dunn & Dunn, 1981).
[b]Total score on a researcher-developed assessment using *The Snowy Day* by Ezra Jack Keats.
[c]Standard score, Wide Range Achievement Test–Revised: Reading (Jastak & Wilkinson, 1984).
[d]Standard score, California Achievement Test: Comprehension (Searle et al., 1992).
***p < .001.

as a simple consequence of the students' need to know meanings of the words in text. Correlations from kindergarten PPVT-R scores to reading comprehension performance are strong across the school years through 10th grade.

This pattern of findings raises many questions. One strong possibility is, of course, that vocabulary in kindergarten is just a proxy for all sorts of other experiences and child capabilities that themselves constitute the explanation for differences in comprehension outcomes. Another is that vocabulary in kindergarten strongly predicts vocabulary in the later grades, which in turn is related to concurrent comprehension skills. Indeed, both of these explanations find some support in the data. As shown in Table 2.4, child kindergarten skills other than vocabulary also show moderate to strong correlations with 4th-, 7th-, and 10th-grade comprehension, although none are stronger than vocabulary. And kindergarten vocabulary scores correlate about as strongly with 4th-, 7th-, and 10th-grade vocabulary as they do with 4th-, 7th-, and 10th-grade comprehension. Thus, we do not have here a mystical impact of 5-year-olds' word knowledge on their much later academic achievement. We do have a picture of considerable stability across time in vocabulary skills and of tight interrelationships among a set of tasks reflecting sophisticated oral language performance and literacy achievement.

The stability of vocabulary and other language and literacy measures across time, as displayed in Table 2.4, deserves some attention in its own right. One view is that such stability is only to be expected—we know that children who arrive at school from low-income homes are unlikely to perform as well as children from

Table 2.4. Correlations between literacy-related scores in kindergarten and reading comprehension and receptive vocabulary in 4th, 7th, and 10th grades ($N = 42$–58)

Kindergarten measures	Reading Comprehension[a]			Receptive Vocabulary[b]		
	4th grade	7th grade	10th grade	4th grade	7th grade	10th grade
Receptive vocabulary[b]	.62***	.69***	.60***	.77***	.63***	.68***
Emergent literacy[c]	.63***	.62***	.56***	.60***	.61***	.55***
Academic language[d]	.56***	.54***	.35*	.66***	.61***	.57***
Narrative production[e]	.46***	.46***	.35*	.28*	.31*	.26

[a]Standard score, California Achievement Test: Comprehension (Searle et al., 1992).
[b]Standard score, Peabody Picture Vocabulary Test–Revised (Dunn & Dunn, 1981).
[c]Total score, Early Childhood Diagnostic Instrument: The Comprehensive Assessment Program (Mason & Stewart, 1989).
[d]Percent of formal definitions on a researcher-developed assessment of definitional skill.
[e]Total score on a researcher-developed assessment of narrative ability, *The Bear Story*.
*p < .05; ***p < .001

middle- or high-income homes (Snow et al., 1998), presumably in part because the skills they bring with them determine to a large extent their ability to profit from opportunities to learn encountered at school. In 2003 and 2005, for example, the average reading score of fourth and eighth graders on National Assessment of Educational Progress standardized tests who were eligible for free or reduced lunch was significantly lower than that of their classmates from middle-income homes, with little improvement in scores over the two assessments (National Center for Education Statistics, 2003; Perie, Grigg, & Donahue, 2005).

We reject social class as an explanation for our findings, however. The well-documented social class differences in language (RAND Reading Study Group, 2002) and reading outcomes are not in dispute, but they are not directly relevant to the pattern of findings we report. First, all of the children in our study came from relatively low-income homes; thus, the differential effects of social class on their performance are minimized. Second, the distribution of the entire group shifted slightly downward in comparison with the norming sample over time, suggesting that as a group these students were slipping below the performance level that could reasonably have been expected of them given their early skills. Third, the students were in widely varying school settings, ranging from demoralized and chaotic urban public schools to well-equipped suburban public schools to strict, academically focused religious and independent schools. The very strong correlations between kindergarten and later measures suggest that the variation in those school settings was largely irrelevant to child outcomes—those who started out with larger vocabularies and better emergent literacy skills ended up as better comprehenders 5, 8, and even 11 years later. Surely that is a worrying finding in a society built around the notion of the common school and committed to holding all students to high standards before providing them with a high school diploma. It is precisely what Rothstein (2004) would have predicted, however.

UNANSWERED QUESTIONS

Our previously published analyses make clear that children who have heard varied vocabulary at home and preschool, who have engaged in book reading and other literacy practices, and who have been exposed to extended discourse are better prepared for the tasks of kindergarten. Where do these findings about predictors to kindergarten skills leave us? First, we clearly want more information about how these children developed over the school years as readers, writers, and, more generally, as students. Science, social studies, even math[2] are very difficult subjects for children who read dysfluently and with poor comprehension. In this book, our first goal is to present longitudinal data on the developmental trajectories of

---

[2] It might seem that reading is implicated in math performance only when children have to solve story problems. In addition, however, much teaching about math presupposes the ability to read accompanying texts, and many opportunities for math reasoning are missed if children cannot read texts in science and social studies.

children from low-income families and to document the continuities and discontinuities in their literacy development from kindergarten through secondary school.

As the students in this study entered the middle and secondary grades, however, it quickly became clear to us that high levels of literacy achievement were not sufficient to ensure their success as students. Some of the better readers and writers in the group were receiving poor grades, being held back, and even contemplating dropping out of school. Not surprisingly, they were also reporting their growing dislike of school and their decreasing ambitions to finish high school and attend college. In order to understand such disconnections between literacy and school success defined more broadly, our second goal is to describe in greater detail how these students experienced school, how they understood its relationship to their long-term goals, and how engaged they were in various aspects of school. We referred to this complex set of understandings, experiences, and goals as "motivational resources," and we sought to understand how information about students' motivational resources could help explain their success or failure in school.

SPECIAL FEATURES OF THIS RESEARCH

The research enterprise reported here differs in a number of ways from previous studies of these same issues. First, as noted previously, we restricted ourselves to children growing up in low-income families, most who were living in urban neighborhoods and attending public or low-cost independent schools. Thus, we selected a group of students who had higher-than-average risks of literacy difficulties and of school failure.

Second, as just noted, we have attempted both to understand these students' literacy development and to place their literacy skills in the broader context of school success. Thus, we have incorporated information about both early developing literacy skills and later motivational resources into our models predicting school success. The bodies of research on literacy and on academic motivation have in general been quite separate; literacy researchers tend to believe that literacy is the primary, if not the only, determinant of school success, and motivation researchers tend to have limited understanding of the complexity of reading development and its crucial role in academic success. Even before we undertook the quantitative analyses described in detail in the next chapter, we became convinced that attending to motivational resources in addition to literacy resources was crucial because unhappy, bored, disconnected, and unmotivated students are unlikely to be making optimal progress in school (Pianta & Walsh, 1996). Understanding students requires knowing about the motivational resources they command as well as the literacy skills they possess.

Third, this is a particularly detailed and data-rich study, in the long period of time over which we followed the participants (from age 3 through 10th grade), in the many kinds of developmental data we collected, and in the careful descriptions of participants' home and preschool environments. Because we collected multiple waves of test data on language and literacy, we could use sophisticated quantitative analyses such as growth modeling to identify predictive relationships. Because we collected wide-ranging test- and self-report data, we could use cluster analyses to see patterns of association across the group. Because we collected extensive interview data from the students, their mothers, and, in some cases, their teachers, as well as writing data from the students themselves, we could formulate a multifaceted understanding of how the students developed and the many forces impinging on their lives.

Thus, in the subsequent chapters of this book we present both multivariate analyses of our entire sample of participants and individual case studies of participants whose development is of particular interest, either because they exemplify larger trends or because they constitute illuminating exceptions. Growth modeling is a technique that is useful in both types of analysis; individual differences in rate of growth on comprehension, the key literacy outcome measure, can be accounted for using intercepts and rates of growth on predictor variables such as vocabulary and word reading. Growth modeling has many strengths as a quantitative tool for data like ours because it is robust against missing data, and the availability of multiple waves of data on individual children means that parameter estimates are highly reliable (Singer & Willett, 2003).

At the same time, growth models can be used to illuminate the progress of individual students who are the subjects of case studies and to compare them with the larger group. Thus, although it is certainly a highly quantified technique, growth modeling can also be used to enrich portraits based primarily on qualitative data.

ORGANIZATION OF THIS BOOK

In the next chapter, we chart continuities and discontinuities in the literacy development of the participants in this study and then go on to ask how three key literacy skills relate to reading comprehension in Grades 4–10 for this group. We explore in that analysis various facets of the stark fact that the knowledge and skills that children take with them into kindergarten strongly predict where they end up as readers in 10th grade. The analyses of the preschool years that is summarized previously describe in considerable detail the types of talk and literacy activities, at home and in preschool settings, which predicted good language outcomes for the children in this group. In other words, we know a lot about how this group of low-income children got to where they were at kindergarten. And we will demonstrate in the next chapter that where they were in kindergarten can explain, statistically, a lot about where they ended up 10 years later. We explore why the kindergarten–middle school connections are so strong, why schools seem not to have reordered children or reduced correlations from kindergarten to later performance to any degree, and how home factors continued to influence students' literacy outcomes. A central issue we focus on in the next chapter is the complexity of reading comprehension—not just as an immediate challenge for the students in the study but also as a construct for researchers in the field of literacy. In the process, we also provide a description of the school and home experiences of these students and a description of their trajectories through adolescence as readers, writers, and learners, with a focus on the degree of continuity observed within those trajectories.

In Chapter 4, we present three case studies of successful, high-performing readers who displayed both early and ongoing success in literacy but whose academic outcomes did not reflect their excellent literacy skills. We explore in those case studies the motivational, interpersonal, and environmental factors that may have led to these students' disappointing progress in the face of their excellent accomplishments as readers and writers.

In Chapter 5, we present data on motivational resources of all the participants in sixth and seventh grades, and we describe how the participants' motivational resources relate to their other characteristics and to their academic outcomes. We conceptualize literacy skills and motivation together as scholastic resources available to students trying to negotiate the tasks of the middle grades. We present a cluster analysis to organize the several dimensions of data available about the students.

In Chapter 6, we present several case studies of students whose resources and trajectories exemplify each of the clusters identified in Chapter 5. Chapters 4 and 6 display the several different pathways on which youth from low-income families can get launched and simultaneously show the many different kinds of information we have available about the students in this study.

In Chapter 7, we reveal a little more about where these students ended up after the last formal data collection had been completed. Finally, in Chapter 8, we connect our findings to policy and practice suggestions designed to improve adolescents' chances of academic success.

3

Early Language and Literacy Skills and Later Reading Comprehension

Literacy Predicts Literacy

If children are to do well in school—if they are to be successful in learning math, biology, and history; in acquiring vocabulary and world knowledge through reading; and in passing the tests that are required for high school graduation, college entry, and employment—they must learn to read with comprehension. Reading comprehension is the central academic skill, the prerequisite to academic success in all domains. And yet, we have relatively little research-based knowledge about how to deliver instruction focused on reading comprehension (Durkin, 1979). In contrast, the research-based knowledge underlying guidelines for instruction focused on word reading is much more robust (National Reading Panel, 2000; Snow et al., 1998).

It is not surprising that earlier reports that found comprehension instruction to be infrequent and inexplicit (RAND Reading Study Group, 2002) appear to apply as well to practices that continue to be used in classrooms (Popplewell & Doty, 2001; Taylor, Pearson, Peterson, & Rodriguez, 2003). Basically, most children have to figure out how to comprehend on their own. Fortunately, many manage to do so. Far too many children, however, even those who perform adequately in facing the literacy demands of the primary grades, end up in the category of struggling comprehenders—able to read for limited purposes but unable to meet the demands of learning from text, of working through texts that include novel words and unfamiliar information, or of reading texts critically. For example, recent NAEP data of long-term trends (National Center for Education Statistics [NCES], 2006) using reading performance-level descriptions found 9-year-old students performing better than ever before (96% able to perform discrete reading tasks and 70% demonstrating partially developed skills and understanding), while 17-year-olds showed scores virtually unchanged over the last three decades (80% demonstrating intermediate reading skills and strategies and only 38% able to understand complicated information).

Thus, it becomes crucial to investigate how students become and stay good comprehenders and which students are likely to struggle with comprehension. Of course, we have ample data from the NAEP and other national data sets answering this question in demographic terms: Children from low-income families, children attending urban schools, children whose parents have low education levels, children from African American and Latino families, and children from non–English-speaking homes are overrepresented in the struggling comprehender group (NCES, 1996; Perie, Grigg, & Donahue, 2005).

Another approach to answering the question is to explore how reading comprehension skill develops in a group of students that represents the array of demographic risks and, in particular, to investigate how variation in comprehension ability is related to earlier-achieved reading accomplishments. That is the approach we take in this chapter.

Fourth grade is popularly cited as the grade at which reading comprehension ("reading to 'learn' ") becomes key. Many would argue that a good reading instruction program focuses on comprehension starting in kindergarten (Hoover & Gough, 1990) and that comprehension is always the criterion for reading success. It is undeniable, however, that starting in about fourth grade, comprehension becomes more obviously the problem. The texts that students are expected to read become more complex because they present information that is relatively unfamiliar in ways that can reduce the likelihood of successful comprehension. Furthermore, most children have mastered the task of reading regular and frequently encountered words by fourth grade, so variation in comprehension attributable to decoding skills is greatly reduced, just as variation associated with the capacity to process complex discourse increases.

One of the major goals motivating the longitudinal study we report on here was to determine which earlier-developing language and literacy skills would predict comprehension in the middle and secondary grades. At the time we undertook this research, relatively little data were available to guide our inquiry. Fortunately, since then, a number of other researchers have cast light on their own versions of this question. We briefly summarize their work in the next section before going on to report our own data relevant to continuity from early to later literacy skills.

PREDICTING READING COMPREHENSION

Reading comprehension clearly involves control over two, more basic component skills: word recognition and language comprehension (RAND Reading Study Group, 2002). In fact, the "simple view of 'reading'" (Hoover & Gough, 1990) essentially explains comprehension as the interaction between written word recognition and oral language comprehension. Alternative views of comprehension argue that capacities of the reader (e.g., knowledge, attention, memory, motivation), characteristics of the text (e.g., complexity, topic, discourse structure), and features of the activity (e.g., skimming versus studying, engagement, reading linear versus hyper-texts) all contribute to the success or failure of comprehension (Storch & Whitehurst, 2002; Whitehurst & Lonigan, 1998). The great majority of research on comprehension has focused on reader variables that relate to comprehension outcomes (see review in RAND Reading Study Group, 2002).

Early Predictors of Comprehension

Research has identified two critical domains of skill in preschoolers that predict later reading outcomes: oral language skills and pre-orthographic skills (phonological processing and knowledge about print; Mason, 1992; Nation & Snowling, 1998; Vellutino, Scanlon, & Tanzman, 1994). These two factors influence different aspects of reading acquisition at different times (Stanovich, Nathan, & Zolman, 1988). The association between oral language—particularly vocabulary—and reading has often been found to be greater for later reading (text comprehension in Grades 4 and later) than for early reading (word reading in the primary grades; Storch & Whitehurst, 2002; Whitehurst, 1997; Whitehurst & Lonigan, 1998). For example, in one study, PPVT-R scores and pseudoword reading were the best predictors of seventh graders' reading comprehension (Stanovich et al., 1988).

Storch and Whitehurst (2002) investigated the relationship of code-related skills (print knowledge, emergent writing, and phonological awareness) and oral language skills (semantic, syntactic, and conceptual knowledge) to reading from preschool to fourth grade in a longitudinal study. Their study revealed that children's oral language skills had a very strong relationship with code-related skills in preschool, although the strength of the relationship weakened progressively until, in Grades 1 and 2, the path between the two skills was no longer statistically significant. However, a very close relationship between word decoding and reading comprehension emerged in the early period of reading acquisition. Nevertheless, students' oral language skills resurfaced as a significant predictor of reading comprehension in Grades 3 and 4.

As children's reading skills progress, their oral language skills, especially vocabulary, become an important resource for reading comprehension. This does not mean that oral language skills play no role in the early word-reading stage of development. In fact, it has been shown that oral language skills have an indirect relationship with code-related skills as early as kindergarten and across the early years of schooling (e.g., Catts, Fey, Tomblin & Zhang, 2002; Catts, Fey, Zhang & Tomblin, 1999). Furthermore, studies show a strong continuity and stability in students' code-related skills and oral language skills (Vellutino, 2003; Vellutino & Scanlon, 2002; Wolf & Katzir-Cohen, 2001).

The key issue is that different aspects of the reading process receive cognitive focus at different points in development. Thus, underlying skills in different areas are of greater or lesser relevance in explaining individual differences at different endpoints. Differences among children in phonological awareness are very important in explaining the ease with which they grasp the alphabetic principle in kindergarten and first grade; however, once children have learned the code, the predictive power of phonological awareness declines. Differences among children in vocabulary knowledge are of only modest relevance to explaining variation in first-grade reading, when even children with small vocabularies know most of the words they encounter in their primers, but these differences are quite important in explaining variation as the texts become more challenging and come to include words some children do not know. Differences in fluency are not as important when children are reading simple sentences and brief passages; however, when the texts that children read are longer, being able to integrate information across the texts requires greater speed and efficiency of processing (Nathan & Stanovich, 1991).

Word Recognition

Word recognition is an important source of individual variation in reading comprehension (National Reading Panel, 2000). Children with poor word recognition skills do poorly in reading comprehension, and children with good word recognition skills do better in reading comprehension. In word recognition, accuracy and fluency are critical to process meaning effectively (Stanovich, 1991). Fluency in word recognition enables readers to access and apply relevant higher thinking skills for comprehension (National Reading Panel, 2000). For example, children who struggle or who are slow to recognize printed words as chunks will expend their cognitive energy on identifying words instead of on the processes central to construction of meaning, such as accessing relevant prior knowledge or critical reasoning (Vellutino, 2003; Vellutino & Scanlon, 2002). Researchers have suggested that fluency extends beyond the word level; efficient and rapid grouping of words in grammatically meaningful chunks is also important for comprehension (Beck & McKeown, 1991; Davis, 1968; Marks, Doctorow, & Wittrock, 1974; McKeown, Beck, Omanson, & Perfetti, 1983). Furthermore, the relationship between reading and word recognition is reciprocal; children who have more practice in reading (as well as spelling and writing) will have better representation of words in memory, which will in turn facilitate accurate and fast recognition of printed words (Nagy & Herman, 1985; Sternberg, 1987).

Oral Language Skills as Predictors of Comprehension

As noted previously in this chapter and in Chapter 2, vocabulary has a robust relationship with comprehension, both concurrently and predictively. Vocabulary is not the only language skill that predicts comprehension outcomes, however. In addition, knowledge of discourse structures relates to comprehension.

Children with larger vocabularies understand text better. Numerous studies have shown a strong, robust, and even causal relationship between vocabulary and reading comprehension (McKeown et al., 1983). Although a main source of vocabulary learning is incidental learning from context (Vellutino, 2003), it has been shown that intensive vocabulary instruction does improve reading comprehension (Duke & Kays, 1998; Vellutino, 2003).

Knowledge of discourse types (narrative, expository texts) is also an important predictor of reading comprehension (Duke & Kays, 1998). Knowledge of the structural and organizational characteristics of different types of discourse differentiates good and poor comprehenders. Good comprehenders tend to have a more sophisticated understanding of various discourse types, which helps good comprehenders interact with texts strategically and construct meaning successfully (Scarborough, Dobrich, & Hager, 1991).

Children's understanding of the purpose and structure of narrative and expository texts varies as a function of amount of exposure. Children who have had rich experiences with oral and written narratives have an implicit understanding of the basic story structure and expect to encounter a beginning, a setting, a conflict, and a resolution. Likewise, children who have experiences with informational texts anticipate the opportunity to gain knowledge about the topic of interest and expect a hierarchical organization of content (Echols et al., 1996).

Sources of Skill Differences

Differences in home environments, for example in frequency of book reading and print exposure, play an important role in generating individual differences in literacy achievement. Scarborough and colleagues (1991) found a significant association between frequency of exposure to literacy-related activities, including book reading during the preschool years, and reading success or problems in Grade 2. In addition, print exposure was found to predict growth in reading comprehension even after controlling for age, recognition memory, and previous cognitive performance in fourth-, fifth-, and sixth-grade children (Stanovich et al., 1996). Furthermore, a study of a group of children followed over 10 years showed that exposure to print in first grade explained variance in growth in reading comprehension through 11th grade (Fuchs, Fuchs, Hosp, & Jenkins, 2001). Inadequate exposure to print can impede development of the vocabulary, background knowledge, and metalinguistic knowledge that are essential for reading comprehension, especially if other possible sources of development, such as exposure to rich conversation and to excellent instruction, are limited.

UNDERSTANDING CONCURRENT AND PREDICTIVE RELATIONSHIPS IN READING DEVELOPMENT

Considerable research has been conducted since the 1970s specifying the skills and capacities that correlate concurrently with reading comprehension. We know that children who comprehend well also possess a variety of other skills and that poor performance in any of a wide number of capabilities, ranging from text memory to vocabulary to syntactic processing to inferencing, can undercut reading comprehension (see RAND Reading Study Group, 2002, for a review).

The studies of concurrent correlations of reading comprehension suggest a number of hypotheses about the developmental predictors of comprehension. We have just reviewed the evidence suggesting that early skills in word reading, vocabulary, and extended discourse relate to later comprehension, but this evidence does not always differentiate "true precursors" from "early indicators." True precursors of comprehension skills are those earlier developing reading skills that help explain differences in comprehension even though concurrent relationships are absent. For example, children who read words inaccurately or slowly are likely to become poor comprehenders (Jastak & Wilkinson, 1984), but, children who start out with low fluency typically remain inaccurate and slow readers. What about inaccurate slow readers who receive effective intervention such that they become accurate and fluent readers? Do they continue nonetheless to lag in comprehension?

In Chapter 2, we presented the surprisingly high correlation in the Home–School Study participants between early vocabulary and later comprehension. We noted, however, that this relationship was probably mediated by vocabulary scores concurrent with the later reading comprehension assessments, which, in turn, were predicted by the earlier vocabulary scores. In other words, early vocabulary scores are an indicator, not a precursor, of later comprehension. Many developmental and instructional events might be expected to disrupt the relationship between kindergarten vocabulary and 10th-grade reading comprehension. The surprise in the findings briefly previewed in Chapter 2 is that, in general, that relationship was not disrupted.

In this chapter, we delve more deeply into the relationships between early emerging and later reading skills by testing whether level and/or growth in hypothesized precursor skills explain growth in reading comprehension ability. Specifically, we focus in this chapter on the following questions:

- What predicts progress in early elementary school language and literacy skills?

- What is the relationship between progress in elementary school language and literacy skills and growth in reading comprehension between 4th grade and 10th grade?

Analyses designed to answer our questions were informed by the findings summarized in Chapter 2 concerning the relationship between home and preschool language and literacy environments and the students' earlier emerging literacy skills. Those results were based entirely on regression analyses. In other words, the analyses were designed to explain variation in child outcome variables measured just once, in kindergarten. Although the analyses were informative, they were also subject to some limitations. Most important, it is extremely difficult to accurately and reliably assess complex child capacities, in particular with young children, on a single occasion. Furthermore, using a single time-point outcome confounds two aspects of children's development—the level at which they are functioning and the speed with which their capacities are changing.

Fortunately, we were able to continue collecting data on our participants after kindergarten. In fact, we collected data on key language and literacy constructs in Grades 1–4, 6, 7, 9, 10 and 12, enabling us to seek relationships between home and preschool predictors and both level and rate of growth in child skills. Multiple waves of measurement of our key constructs can be analyzed to provide information about the development of language and literacy skills. By using individual growth modeling, we were able to determine not only each child's ability in relation to other participants in the study or to national norms but also how children's scores in each of these areas changed over time and whether or not there were systematic predictors of these changes.

Methods

Participants

Participants in the Home–School Study were, as described in Chapter 2, originally recruited through Head Start and other early childhood centers serving low-income families when the children were 3 years old. Although a number of participants dropped out of the study over the years, demographic characteristics of successive analytic samples suggest that attrition was not biased (see Chapter 2, Table 2.1). In addition, growth modeling used for these analyses is flexible with regards to missing data.

Measures

In these analyses, we analyzed four outcome variables for which we had multiple waves of data included (see Table 3.1).

1. *Receptive Vocabulary.* Raw scores on the PPVT-R (Dunn & Dunn, 1981) constituted our measure of receptive vocabulary. Because we had scores at Grades 2, 4, and 6, we could estimate growth trajectories for raw scores on this test for the 68 children for whom multiple waves of data were available in order then to analyze what home and school variables predicted intercept and rate of growth in receptive vocabulary.

2. *Academic Language.* Our measure of academic language reflected the use of formal definitional syntax and content on a task of giving meanings for 10 common nouns (see Kurland & Snow, 1997, for previous growth analyses on these data). Children completed this task each year from kindergarten through fourth grade. Sufficient waves of data were available to estimate growth models for 59 children.

Table 3.1. Measures of central tendency and variation on raw scores of the language and literacy assessments, with corresponding percentile scores

	Mean raw score	Mean raw SD	Raw score range	Mean percentile score
PPVT-R[a]				
Kindergarten (*n* = 75)	59.68	15.35	33–101	36.30
2nd grade (*n* = 66)	90.92	12.30	62–117	46.67
4th grade (*n* = 59)	107.25	12.96	81–141	50.92
6th grade (*n* = 57)	118.75	13.65	98–154	44.35
Academic Language				
Kindergarten (n = 75)	3.00	4.44	0–14	n/a
1st grade (n = 70)	3.89	4.76	0–13	n/a
2nd grade (n = 64)	8.73	4.62	0–14	n/a
3rd grade (n = 63)	7.41	2.63	0–10	n/a
4th grade (n = 58)	7.98	2.05	1–10	n/a
WRAT-R[b]				
1st grade (*n* = 65)	43.03	10.49	24–66	47.11
2nd grade (*n* = 41)	56.05	8.77	37–72	37.97
4th grade (*n* = 58)	69.97	9.70	39–93	51.83

	Mean grade equivalent score	Mean grade equivalent SD	Grade equivalent range	Mean percentile score
CAT[c]				
4th grade (*n* = 57)	4.60	1.92	1.40–11.00	46.25
7th grade (*n* = 54)	7.51	2.77	2.20–12.90	51.19
10th grade (*n* = 41)	9.96	2.65	2.30–12.90	51.51

[a]Dunn & Dunn (1981)
[b]Jastak & Wilkinson (1984)
[c]Searle, Casella, & McCulloch (1992)

3. *Word Recognition.* We administered the Wide-Range Achievement Test–Revised (WRAT-R; Jastak & Wilkinson, 1984) during school visits at Grades 1, 2, and 4. Individual growth was modeled using the raw scores of 55 children.

4. *Reading Comprehension.* We used the Reading Comprehension measure from the California Achievement Test: Comprehension, 5th Edition (CAT; Searle, Casella, & McCulloch, 1992). This test was administered to students in Grades 4, 7, and 10. Students read narrative and expository passages silently and then respond to a series of multiple-choice questions based on the reading. Students attempt to complete all 50 questions in the allotted 50-minute time period. Unlike the WRAT-R and PPVT-R, students are not given the same exact test each year. Instead, grade-level tests contain a unique set of

passages for each grade level assessed. Thus, the use of raw scores would not necessarily provide us with a valid measure of growth. For growth modeling of the CAT, we choose to use grade-equivalent scores of the 52 students in order to determine whether they were performing at grade level across test administrations.

Table 3.1 gives means and standard deviations for all of our key analytic variables for each of the ages at which the tests were administered. As would be expected, student raw scores increased with grade promotion for the PPVT-R, the academic language measure, and the WRAT-R. Similarly, average CAT scores for the participants appeared to rise concurrently with grade promotion. However, a closer look reveals the vast range in scores, whereby some students remained at an early elementary level in reading comprehension well into high school, whereas high performing students hit ceiling on the measure by seventh grade.

The final column of Table 3.1 presents the percentile scores, where available, for these same measures. As a group, the students tended to score at or slightly below the population mean on all measures at all ages. Some evidence suggested improvement relative to the general population through 4th grade on the PPVT-R and through 10th grade on the CAT.

The preschool composite measures introduced in the previous chapter—Maternal Extended Discourse, Maternal Rare Word Density, Home Support for Literacy, Teacher Extended Discourse, Classroom Exposure to Rare Words, and Classroom Curriculum—were used as control measures in this analysis.

Analysis

In order to fully investigate the Matthew effect, that is, the rate at which students who start off behind fall further behind, we first fit models of growth over time in receptive vocabulary, academic language, word recognition, and reading comprehension using SAS PROC MIXED (Singer & Willett, 2003). Using individual growth modeling, we were able to establish estimated initial status for individual children and for the sample on average, parameter estimates that are conceptually and statistically similar to the outcomes in our previous regression analyses but estimated with greater reliability. This approach also allows us to estimate within-person and between-person rates of growth as predicted by time and early home and preschool experiences. The regression analyses described in Chapter 1 represent a limited strategy for analyzing longitudinal data in that they describe how the participants fared on average at kindergarten based on mean sample scores of previously collected preschool measures. With individual growth modeling, we are able to estimate each child's trajectory of change on our language and literacy measures, as long as we have at least three waves of data. A method such as repeated measures analysis of variance (ANOVA) can provide information on group mean differences in scores at different time points as a function of time and other predictors, but is likely to confound true change with measurement error because it does not incorporate terms reflecting individual differences in rate of growth.

The first step in a growth model analysis is to fit individual models to the data from each child. These are called 'level-1 models.' For the level-1 component of the growth model for PPVT-R, for instance, we fit the following within-person model for child j at time i:

$$\text{PPVT-R}_{ij}\text{hat} = \pi_{0j} + \pi_{1j}(\text{GRADE})_{ij} + r_{ij} \quad \text{where } r_{ij} \sim N(0,\sigma^2)$$

Observed growth trajectories for each child across all the waves of data collection are constructed by plotting scores for PPVT-R at each time point data is collected. Thus, an intercept (π_{0j}) representing predicted PPVT-R for the child at kindergarten (initial status) and a slope (π_{1j}) representing the predicted rate of change in PPVT-R at data collection intervals (every other year in this example) is estimated for each participant in order to determine whether there is a significant effect of time. Raw scores rather than standardized scores are used in order to examine observed growth rather than ranking of the individual relative to national norms.

The second step is to develop a level-2 model in which all of the individual growth models are analyzed together to see what accounts for differences among them in starting point and in rate of growth. In the level-2 component of the growth model for PPVT-R, we test whether there are between-person differences in rates of change that can be explained by predictors other than time. In this example, to test whether exposure to rare words in the homes of preschool-age children are related to PPVT-R growth, we fit the model:

$$\pi_{0j} = \beta_{00} + \beta_{01} (\text{MATERNAL RARE WORD DENSITY}) + u_{0j} \quad \text{where}$$
$$\pi_{1j} = \beta_{10} + \beta_{11} (\text{MATERNAL RARE WORD DENSITY}) + u_{1j} \quad \left(\frac{u_{0j}}{u_{1j}} \right) \sim N(0s,\tau)$$

This level-2 model tests for a relationship between the predictor, exposure to rare words, and the child's initial status (π_{0j}) and rate of change (π_{1j}) in PPVT-R. For our analyses we assume a linear effect of time. In those cases in which we only had three waves of data, we did not have enough information to test more complicated growth trajectories. In those cases in which we did have more than three waves of data, we saw no evidence for anything other than a linear relationship to time.

In addition to fitting models of early language and literacy skills (receptive vocabulary, academic language, word recognition) and exploring the factors that explained differences among children on these measures, we also fit estimated trajectories in reading comprehension for participants as they moved from elementary school (4th grade) to middle school (7th grade) to high school (10th grade). However, we used the patterns of change from the early language and literacy growth models as predictors in the reading comprehension models. In other words, vocabulary, academic language, and word recognition were used as time-varying predictors in the analysis of reading comprehension growth, thus incorporating children's initial status in each of these variables as well as their rate of change into the models. Using multilevel modeling to represent within-person and between-person change allowed us to include patterns of nonstatic variables among our predictors.

Our first aim was to test the hypothesis that children's scores on vocabulary, academic language, and word recognition increase over time and that children grow at different rates on these measures. Once that was established, our model enabled us to test the potential effects of both initial level (intercept) and rate of growth (slope) in skill in each of these areas on later growth in reading comprehension.

RESULTS FROM GROWTH MODEL ANALYSES

Receptive Vocabulary

For this model and each subsequent growth model, time is represented by grade in school. The time variable was coded as "0" for the first wave of data collected; thus, the intercept in each model describes average score at initial status. Using SAS PROC MIXED to model growth in PPVT-R, we found a straightforward relationship between grade (data collected at kindergarten and Grades 2, 4, and 6) and expansion of receptive vocabulary (see Figure 3.1 and Table 3.2), such that children's vocabulary skill increased in each successive school year.

- *Model 1: Unconditional model.* The trajectory of growth in receptive vocabulary is established by estimating the intercept (PPVT-R score at kindergarten) and the slope (the rate of change over second through sixth grades) in a level-

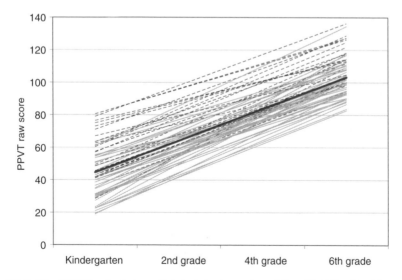

Figure 3.1. PPVT-R estimated growth trajectories by grade and Rare Word Density at home. (*Key:* ——— = PPVT trajectory predicted by mean Rare Word Density; ------ = trajectories of individual students who scored above the mean in Rare Word Density; ——— = trajectories of individual students who scored below the mean in Rare Word Density.)

Table 3.2. Estimates of fixed and random effects from a series of fitted individual growth models in which time and preschool composites from home and school predict the initial level of vocabulary (PPVT-R; kindergarten) and rate of change in vocabulary through grade 6 (*n* = 68)

	Parameter estimate (*SE*)			
	Model 1	Model 2	Model 3	Model 4
Fixed effects				
Intercept	44.59***	4.06	46.32***	17.33*
	(1.86)	(6.74)	(1.74)	(7.44)
Time (grade)	19.54***	19.37***	19.40***	19.29***
	(0.51)	(0.51)	(0.53)	(0.52)
Home environmental factors at preschool age				
Maternal				
Extended Discourse		0.01		
		(0.02)		
Home Support for Literacy		0.95***		0.63*
		(0.26)		(0.26)
Rare Word Density		0.21***		0.16***
		(0.04)		(0.04)
Preschool environmental factors				
Teacher Extended Discourse			4.77***	3.18**
			(1.27)	(1.12)
Classroom Exposure to Rare Words			3.56***	1.83~
			(1.06)	(1.00)
Classroom curriculum			1.44	
			(1.10)	
Random effects (variance components)				
Intercept (1,1)	131.15***	58.53***	71.40***	49.05***
Residual	80.03***	75.79***	77.26***	76.86***
AIC	1993.6	1816.2	1735.4	1724.3

Note: SAS PROC MIXED Procedure indicated that the random effect of the slope variance component was estimated to be zero (Estimated G matrix not positive definite) in initial analyses. Although there is a likely random effect in the population, it cannot be estimated with this sample, thus the model was fit without including the command to estimate the random effect of the slope. (See Stahl and Fairbanks [1986] for more about variance components.)

~$p < .10$; *$p < .05$; **$p < .01$; ***$p < .001$.

1 (within-person) model. On average, students had a raw score of 45.2 on their kindergarten PPVT-R and made gains of 19.5 points every 2 years. Significant variation occurred in the baseline score for receptive vocabulary (intercept) that could be further explained by level-2 (between-person) modeling. However, there was not a significant variation in the rate of growth (slope); in other words, the students all made gains over time at the same rate.

- *Model 2: Home environmental factors at preschool age.* Between-person differences in the composites Home Support for Literacy and Maternal Rare Word Density at home explained significant variance in the PPVT-R intercept. Children who had experienced greater Home Support for Literacy and who had been exposed to higher Maternal Rare Word Density had higher PPVT-R scores (see Figure 3.1). Tests showed no interactions between time and any of the home environmental variables.

- *Model 3: Preschool environmental factors.* Three composite measures of preschool literacy environment were included in this model. Teacher Extended Discourse and Classroom Exposure to Rare Words at preschool explained a significant proportion of difference in the PPVT-R intercept. Tests showed no interactions between time and any of the preschool environmental variables.

- *Model 4: Combining home and school environmental factors.* The two significant home composite measures and the two significant school composite measures were included in this model. All four composites were significantly related to the intercept.

All of the children experienced positive gains in PPVT-R scores over time and all at essentially the same rate. In our hierarchical model building, we found that the following four indicators of the children's experience during the preschool years all contributed uniquely to explaining initial level of vocabulary skill: Home Support for Literacy, Maternal Rare Word Density, Teacher Extended Discourse, and Classroom Exposure to Rare Words.

Academic Language

SAS PROC MIXED was again used to fit a series of hierarchical models of growth in definitional skill.

- *Model 1: Unconditional model.* The trajectory of growth in definitional skill is established by estimating the intercept (academic language score at kindergarten) and the slope (the rate of yearly change through fourth grade) in a level-1 (within-person) model. Kindergarten scores showed a floor effect in that more than half of the participants scored 0, which meant that they were unable to provide a formal definition for any of the test words. In order to make the parameter estimate of the intercept easier to interpret, time was recentered at first grade, when most students were able to produce at least one definition. Although recentering does not change the structure of the model, it uses all available data, maintains identical slope estimates and goodness-of-fit statistics, and can provide a more meaningful interpretation of initial status (Singer & Willett, 2003). On average, students had a raw score of 3.71 on their first-grade academic language score and made gains of 1.4 points every year. There was significant variation in both the baseline score for academic language (intercept) and in rate of growth (slope) that could be further explained by level-2 (between-person) modeling.

- *Model 2: Home environmental factors at preschool age.* Composites reflecting children's home language and literacy environments at ages 3–5 were included in the model. Home Support for Literacy was significantly related to growth in academic language.

- *Model 3: Preschool environmental factors.* Three composite measures reflecting the preschool language and literacy environment were included in this model. Classroom Exposure to Rare Words explained a significant proportion of difference in growth of academic language.

- *Model 4: Combining home and school environmental factors.* In this model, the significant composite measures from home and school were included together. Home Support for Literacy remained as a significant predictor of academic language in the final model, whereas Classroom Exposure to Rare Words approached significance at $p < .06$.

Although a few children showed a decrease in academic language over time, on average, children's skill increased as they moved from kindergarten through fourth grade (see Figure 3.2 and Table 3.3).

Word Recognition

Again using SAS PROC MIXED for growth modeling, we found a significant positive effect of time on WRAT-R scores. Students were assessed on the WRAT-R at first, second, and fourth grades. Although there was a considerable amount of missing data at the second grade administration (19 of the 55 cases in the model),

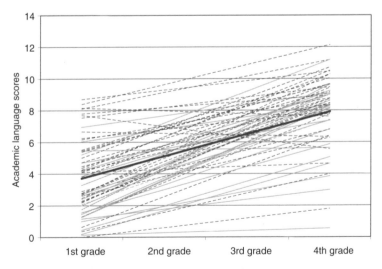

Figure 3.2. Academic Language estimated growth trajectories by grade and Home Support for Literacy. (*Key:* ——— = Academic Language trajectory predicted by mean Home Support for Literacy; ------ = trajectories of individual students who scored above the mean in Home Support for Literacy; ——— = trajectories of individual students who scored below the mean in Home Support for Literacy.)

Table 3.3. Estimates of fixed and random effects from a series of fitted individual growth models in which time and preschool composites from home and school predict the initial level of academic language (definitions; kindergarten) and rate of change in academic language through 4th grade ($n = 65$) with time centered at first grade

	Parameter estimate (SE)			
	Model 1	Model 2	Model 3	Model 4
Fixed effects				
Intercept	3.71***	−2.83~	3.80***	−0.79
	(0.45)	(1.48)	(0.30)	(1.46)
Time	1.40***	1.36***	1.35***	1.35***
(1st grade centered)	(0.10)	(0.10)	(0.10)	(0.10)
Home environmental factors at preschool age				
Maternal				
Extended Discourse		0.01		
		(0.01)		
Home Support				
for Literacy		0.16**		0.18**
		(0.05)		(0.05)
Rare Word				
Density		0.01~		
		(0.01)		
Preschool environmental factors				
Teacher Extended				
Discourse			0.24	
			(0.28)	
Classroom Exposure				
to Rare Words			0.50*	0.41~
			(0.23)	(0.21)
Classroom				
Curriculum			0.20	
			(0.24)	
Random effects (variance components)				
Intercept (1,1)	6.37**	3.80*	4.39*	3.94*
	(2.26)	(1.91)	(2.11)	(1.96)
Slope (2,2)	0.09	0.07	0.07	0.07
	(0.12)	(0.12)	(0.12)	(0.12)
Residual	4.90***	5.02***	5.04***	5.04***
	(0.52)	(0.55)	(0.55)	(0.55)
AIC	1411.6	1347.7	1317.6	1312.3

~$p < .10$; *$p < .05$; **$p < .01$; ***$p < .001$.

SAS PROC MIXED is robust enough to handle this missing data and estimate trajectories for these students.

- *Model 1: Unconditional model.* The trajectory of growth in word recognition skill is established by estimating the intercept (WRAT-R score at first grade) and the slope (the rate of change through three time periods) in a level-1 (within-person) model. On average, students had a raw score of 30.6 on their first-grade WRAT-R score and made gains of 13.1 points between each two successive assessments. (SAS PROC MIXED allows for uneven intervals of data in estimation of trajectories.) Significant variation occurred in the baseline score for the WRAT-R (intercept) and in rate of growth (slope) that could be further explained by level-2 (between-person) modeling.

- *Model 2: Home environmental factors at preschool age.* Composites reflecting home environmental factors collected when children were in preschool were included in the model. Home Support for Literacy was significantly related to growth in word recognition.

- *Model 3: Preschool environmental factors.* Three composite measures of preschool literacy environment were included in this model. Classroom Exposure to Rare Words explained a significant proportion of difference in growth of word recognition, while Teacher Extended Discourse approached significance.

- *Model 4: Combining home and school environmental factors.* In this model, the nonsignificant composite measures from home and school were removed. On average, students' scores increased as they progressed through elementary school (see Figure 3.3 and Table 3.4), with Classroom Exposure to Rare Words positively related to early growth in word recognition. Home Support for Literacy and Teacher Extended Discourse were no longer significant when controlling for Classroom Exposure to Rare Words.

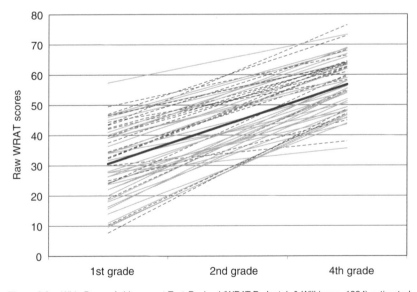

Figure 3.3. Wide Range Achievement Test-Revised (WRAT-R; Jastak & Wilkinson, 1984) estimated growth trajectories by grade and exposure to Rare Words in the Preschool Classroom (*Key:* ——— = WRAT trajectory predicted by mean Exposure to Rare Words; ------ = trajectories of individual students who scored above the mean in Exposure to Rare Words; ——— = trajectories of individual students who scored below the mean in Exposure to Rare Words.)

Table 3.4. Estimates of fixed and random effects from a series of fitted individual growth models in which time and preschool composites from home and school predict the initial level of word recognition (WRAT-R; first grade) and rate of change in word recognition through elementary school ($n = 55$)

	Parameter estimate (SE)			
	Model 1	Model 2	Model 3	Model 4
Fixed effects				
Intercept	30.58***	9.43	30.68***	20.98**
	(1.56)	(6.47)	(1.54)	(6.41)
Time (grade)	13.11***	13.12***	13.15***	13.14***
	(0.52)	(0.52)	(0.52)	(0.66)
Home environmental factors at preschool age				
Maternal Extended Discourse		0.03		
		(0.02)		
Home Support for Literacy		0.49*		0.37
		(0.24)		(0.24)
Rare Word Density		0.04		
		(0.04)		
Preschool environmental factors				
Teacher Extended Discourse			1.87~	1.54
			(1.04)	(1.01)
Classroom Exposure to Rare Words			2.84**	2.64**
			(0.88)	(0.87)
Classroom Curriculum			0.47	
			(0.90)	
Random effects (variance components)				
Intercept (1,1)	115.56***	113.94***	110.84***	111.56***
	(27.45)	(27.61)	(27.27)	(27.42)
Slope (2,2)	8.69**	8.74**	8.62**	8.53**
	(3.19)	(3.19)	(3.17)	(3.15)
Residual	11.67***	11.64***	11.73***	11.78***
	(2.86)	(2.85)	(2.87)	(2.88)
AIC	1010.6	1011.1	988.4	988.9

~$p < .10$; *$p < .05$; **$p < .01$; ***$p < .001$.

The picture that emerges from the growth modeling analysis extends the previous findings from the regression analysis in powerful ways. First, for the one construct that was identical across the two analyses—receptive vocabulary—much the same picture emerged from both. Exposure to rare words at home and at school, as well as to Teacher Extended Discourse, were significant predictors of baseline vocabulary in the growth analysis, just as they had been of kindergarten scores in the regression.

In the regression analysis predicting kindergarten narrative performance (an indicator of academic language), Home Support for Literacy was a significant predictor. Home Support for Literacy was also associated with growth in the measure of academic language analyzed here, giving definitions. In addition, Classroom Exposure to Rare Words predicted growth in definitions, although it was not associated with kindergarten performance in narratives. Whereas both narratives and definitions are indicators of academic language skills, those two performances also call on genre-specific knowledge. In particular, quality of definitions is likely to be related to vocabulary knowledge, whereas narrative skill is less dependent on sophisticated vocabulary.

Growth in word recognition was most powerfully predicted by Classroom Exposure to Rare Words—a variable that was also, somewhat surprisingly, strongly related to kindergarten emergent literacy scores. Thus, we see that experiences during the preschool years that are related to vocabulary status at kindergarten also explain growth in word reading.

Having explored the predictors during the preschool period of both kindergarten literacy outcomes and growth during the elementary years in literacy measures, we turn to the burning issue in literacy development: What explains success in reading comprehension? In our final growth analysis, we address that question, exploring how these earlier emerging language and literacy skills relate to the development of comprehension during the middle and secondary grades for this group of students.

Predicting Reading Comprehension

- *Model 1: Unconditional model.* The trajectory of growth in reading comprehension is established by estimating the intercept (CAT score at 4th grade) and the slope (the rate of change over 7th and 10th grades) in a level-1 (within-person) model. On average, students had a predicted grade-equivalent score of 2.14 (start of second grade) on their fourth-grade CAT and predicted growth of 2.53 grade levels every 3 years. Although this predicted intercept is somewhat lower than the simple mean calculation for the participants' CAT scores at fourth grade, our model is taking into account measurement of CAT scores over time and individual trajectories in computing this estimate. Estimates of the random effects indicated variation in the baseline score for comprehension (intercept) and in rate of growth (slope) that could be further explained by level-2 (between-person) modeling.

- *Model 2: Early reading progress.* Scores over time on the WRAT-R and academic language were included in the model as time-varying predictors. As noted previously, inter-individual variation in PPVT-R growth was extremely limited, so there was relatively little scope for such variation to explain change on the CAT. Thus, we chose to include the raw PPVT-R score at kindergarten only instead of PPVT-R as a time-varying predictor. Person-level change in the WRAT-R and academic language, and PPVT-R raw score at kindergarten explained significant variance in CAT trajectories.

- *Model 3: Home environmental factors at preschool age.* Three composite measures of home environment collected during the preschool time period were included in this model. Home Support for Literacy and Maternal Extended Discourse explained a significant proportion of change in the CAT over time, while Maternal Rare Word Density was not significantly related to growth in comprehension.

- *Model 4: Preschool environmental factors.* Three composite measures of preschool literacy environment were included in this model. Teacher Extended Discourse and Classroom Exposure to Rare Words explained a significant proportion of change in CAT over time, while the Classroom Curriculum composite was unrelated to growth in reading comprehension.

- *Models 5: Combining early progress and home and school environmental factors.* For this model, significant time-varying predictors of growth (i.e., change in the WRAT-R and academic language, as well as our static measure of PPVT-R at kindergarten), were included along with Home Support for Literacy, Maternal Extended Discourse, Teacher Extended Discourse, and Classroom Exposure to Rare Words. Although both the home and preschool predictors were significantly related to comprehension on their own, they dropped out of the model when included with early skills in reading, most likely a result of covariance with those measures. Further, when all variables were included in the model together, the random effect of the intercept could not be estimated. Thus, model 2 appears to be our best explanation of growth in comprehension skills.

Growth modeling shows that early progress in literacy skills—word recognition and academic language—is positively related to growth in comprehension as students move through middle school and high school. Because there is so little variation in vocabulary growth among our participants, it does not emerge as an important predictor of later comprehension growth when controlling for other predictors. However, the vocabulary score with which students enter kindergarten is a significant predictor of growth in reading comprehension (see Figure 3.4 and Table 3.5). In addition, although environmental factors were related to growth in early literacy skills, environmental factors were no longer significant predictors of comprehension when controlling for those same literacy skills.

DISCUSSION

The most striking finding from the analyses presented in this chapter is the high degree of continuity from early to later literacy accomplishments. The growth

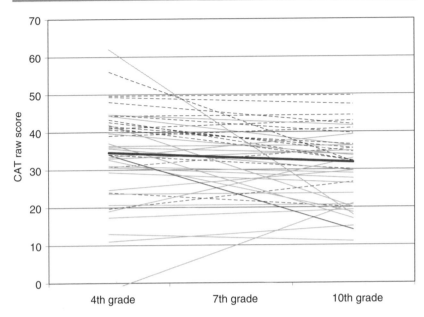

Figure 3.4. Estimated California Achievement Test (CAT; Searle, Casella, & McCulloch, 1992) comprehension trajectories by grade and Peabody Picture Vocabulary Test–Revised (PPVT-R; Dunn & Dunn, 1981) score at Kindergarten. (*Key:* ——— = CAT comprehension trajectory predicted by mean PPVT-R score at Kindergarten; - - - - - - = trajectories of individual students who scored above the mean on the PPVT-R; ——— = trajectories of individual students who scored below the mean on the PPVT-R.)

analysis shows that growth in word recognition and definition skills during the early elementary grades predicts a high percentage of the variance in level of reading comprehension achieved during the later elementary and high school years. Individual differences in growth in vocabulary during those same early years do not explain variation in reading comprehension—probably because there was very little variability in vocabulary growth. Vocabulary scores in kindergarten, however, remain a powerful predictor of reading comprehension level, even when other factors are included in the model as control variables. In fact, when controlling for growth in word recognition and academic language, only vocabulary skill level at the start of school (and not growth in vocabulary over time) was a significant predictor of later comprehension growth.

Lack of variability across children in vocabulary growth could be seen as a reflection of the Matthew effect—that kindergarten vocabulary determines too much of the course of later literacy growth to allow for much in the way of deviation from the trajectory originally set. It is striking that recognizing words and giving formal definitions, in contrast, do show enough variation in developmental trajectories that their growth emerges as significant in predicting reading comprehension. Both word recognition and definitions are bounded skills; they are

Table 3.5. Estimates of fixed and random effects from a series of fitted individual growth models in which time, early reading progress (growth in WRAT-R and definitions), PPVT-R at kindergarten, and preschool composites from home and school predict the initial grade equivalent level of reading comprehension (CAT; fourth grade) and rate of change in reading comprehension grade equivalent through middle school and high school ($n = 52$)

	Parameter estimate (*SE*)				
	Model 1	Model 2	Model 3	Model 4	Model 5
Fixed effects					
Intercept	2.14***	−3.79***	-4.31**	2.23***	−3.64*
	(0.33)	(0.81)	(1.49)	(0.30)	(1.39)
Time (grade)	2.53***	1.53***	2.57***	2.58***	1.79***
	(0.15)	(0.28)	(0.16)	(0.16)	(0.30)
Early reading progress and skills					
WRAT-R Growth		0.07***			0.06**
(1st, 2nd, 4th grades)		(0.02)			(0.02)
Academic Language		0.13*			0.10~
growth (K, 1st, 2nd grades)		(0.05)			(0.06)
PPVT-R at		0.06***			0.04***
kindergarten only		(0.01)			(0.01)
Home environmental factors *at preschool age*					
Maternal Extended Discourse			0.01*		0.003
			(0.004)		(0.003)
Home Support for Literacy			0.14*		0.02
			(0.06)		(0.04)
Rare Word Density			0.01		
			(0.01)		
Preschool environmental factors					
Teacher Extended Discourse				0.72**	0.19
				(0.23)	(0.19)
Classroom Exposure to Rare Words				0.72**	0.24
				(0.19)	(0.17)
Classroom Curriculum				0.06	
				(0.20)	
Random effects *(variance components)*					
Intercept (1,1)	2.70*	0.002	2.06~	1.08	#
	(1.34)	(1.47)	(1.29)	(1.15)	
Slope (2,2)	0.28	0.19	0.33	0.37	0.17
	(0.17)	(0.36)	(0.31)	(0.33)	(0.20)
Residual	1.38**	1.69***	1.34***	1.35***	1.62***
	(0.30)	(0.48)	(0.30)	(0.30)	(0.29)
AIC	629.1	485.1	598.1	561.1	460.9

\# In Model 5, SAS PROC MIXED unable to estimate random effects of intercept for sample.
~$p < .10$; *$p < .05$; **$p < .01$; ***$p < .001$.

not simple to acquire but, nonetheless, are relatively well defined and finite. Thus, they are susceptible to instruction and can easily be affected by variation in quality and intensity of instruction.

Of course, vocabulary is massively influenced by conditions of the environment, as our preschool data show, but vocabulary may not be much influenced by the limited variation in quality or quantity of instruction extant in American schools. In fact, meta-analyses of vocabulary instruction suggest that effective instruction can generate, at most, knowledge of 300 or so extra words a year (Stahl & Fairbanks, 1986)—hardly enough to compensate for differences across children of thousands of words at kindergarten entry. Vocabulary is a much larger domain than either word recognition or definitions, so big jumps in vocabulary knowledge are unlikely to result from a year or two of even relatively good instruction.

It is also worth noting that we could explain a lot of the variance in initial reading comprehension level in 4th grade but rather little in reading comprehension growth between 4th and 10th grades. Again, this finding might well reflect the workings of the Matthew effect: If there is very high continuity from early to later literacy skills, then the differential influences of different classrooms, different schools, or different home environments on later skills will be limited. The claim of the Matthew effect hypothesis is precisely that the literacy-relevant skills children take to school with them determine their later developmental trajectories more powerfully than variation in instruction. We see evidence in support of this hypothesis from our analyses. Variation in children's reading comprehension levels (the intercept) was a product of earlier literacy skills, and even students in the best schools did not stand out as much more rapid learners of reading comprehension skills than those in the worst schools.

Fourth-grade reading comprehension scores were highly correlated in this group with reading comprehension scores at 7th and 10th grades, providing yet another source of support for the claim of continuity in literacy development.

IMPLICATIONS

The robust continuity in literacy skills we report here has two sets of implications. One set has to do with the urgency of exploiting those continuities by improving the language and literacy environments of young children so that they enter school ready to profit rather than suffer from the workings of the Matthew effect. We have good descriptions of the qualities of early childhood programs and early childhood teachers that can generate rich language and emergent literacy environments for children (McGee & Richgels, 2003). We also know a good deal about parent education and intervention programs that enhance the language and literacy environments of young children's homes. For example, the Early Head Start Research and Evaluation Project (2002) demonstrated positive impacts on both parenting behaviors and on child outcomes of intervening with families of children younger than age 3. The Project EASE intervention, designed to

promote parent–child language of precisely the kind found to predict good outcomes in this study, showed significant impacts on kindergarten-age children
(Jordan, Snow, & Porche, 2000). Intervening early to improve the level of skills
children have in kindergarten could be a very efficient and economical way of
improving reading outcomes.

A second set of implications is that we should be working to undermine and
reverse the Matthew effect by increasing the impact of instructional experiences.
There is no excuse for simply letting children who arrive at school with a slight
lag in vocabulary or emergent literacy skills fall farther and farther behind their
classmates. Even if Rothstein (2004) is correct that social class differences in
readiness to learn are too endemic to be completely eliminated, minimizing rather
than exacerbating those differences is certainly a reasonable goal. Schooling needs
to be reorganized so that children who arrive at kindergarten with the weakest
skills have the best chances of receiving excellent instruction from highly trained
teachers. Under the current mechanisms for funding schools, distributing teachers, and selecting literacy programs, lags in early language and literacy skills are
particularly likely to condemn children to long-term failure.

4

Continuities in Literacy, Discontinuities in Outcome

Middle and High School

In Chapter 3, we document the evidence that the Home–School Study students' early reading skills (word recognition, academic language, and receptive vocabulary) were highly predictive of their later reading comprehension skills. In addition, we show that the students' scores on standardized measures of language and literacy ability were highly correlated over time; that is, even as students improved in reading, where they started out in kindergarten predicted much about their progress through school. It is precisely because of the high stakes of early achievement that educational policy has placed such a strong emphasis on kindergarten through third-grade literacy instruction (e.g., NCLB). However, mastery of these necessary skills still may not be sufficient to ensure the later academic success of children from low-income homes as they move through adolescence. In this chapter, we use case studies to explore academic trajectories of students whose literacy skills led us to expect that they would achieve academic success but whose actual outcomes fell far short of expectations.

Based on demographic factors, all of the students in the Home–School Study were at relatively high risk for not completing high school. Recent national statistics (National Center for Education Statistics, 2001) show that children whose families are in the bottom 20% of the U.S. population in annual income are six times more likely to drop out of high school than are their more affluent peers. In addition, children from racial and ethnic minority backgrounds are more likely to drop out, as are boys compared with girls. High school completion rates (including students earning GEDs) were shown to fluctuate between 85% and 87% during the time our participants were entering high school (National Center for Education Statistics, 2001). However, high school completion rates are poor markers for actual dropout statistics because of the way the data are com-

piled, and even this more generous accounting of high school dropout reflects little improvement in graduation trends (Orfield, 2004). When we located the
Home–School Study participants in the year they should have been 12th graders,
30% had either dropped out of school or had been retained in grade 2 years or
more. These retained students have little likelihood of ever completing high
school, especially because Massachusetts has legislated passage of a state examination as an additional high school graduation requirement.

But *risk* means *probability*, not *certainty*, and we were greatly cheered by
finding, as we tested our participants in fourth, sixth, and seventh grades, that
many of them were performing adequately in literacy skills, and some were
extremely advanced. Based on the scores on the assessment battery we administered, only about 20% of our participants might have been expected to have real
academic difficulties. But a much higher proportion encountered difficulties in
the later elementary and middle school grades. Thus, the difficult transition to
middle school for some Home–School Study participants was also a transition for
us, as researchers, as we came to understand that several of our standout elementary students were not succeeding in middle school, even though they surpassed
expectations for literacy skills. We wanted to know why this might be.

To further examine continuities and discontinuities in adolescent literacy
outcomes, we tested relations between literacy assessments and more general academic progress markers for the group. Within the context of those findings, we
developed in-depth case studies of three focal students to illuminate the socio-
emotional processes having the potential to maintain or disrupt the early promise of successful academic trajectories.

THREE CASE STUDIES

We present embedded case studies (Scholz & Tietje, 2001) of three students—
James, Ethan, and Rashida[1]—relying on material gathered from interviews with
them, their parents, and their teachers, as well as from their test results and academic records. We identified these three students early on as being very likely to
succeed academically based on their consistently high performance on standardized assessments and their success in the early grades. But in middle and high
school, these students started to have academic problems and show early indicators of risk for dropout: poor grades, retention in grade, behavioral problems, and
excessive absences.

In addition to the interview material, we examine correlations among literacy assessments at various points in the students' school career, teacher expectations, and grade point averages, and we present these three students' growth
trajectories on several literacy measures. These growth analyses were designed to
highlight simple patterns of growth (or decline) based on time alone and are presented for illustration purposes rather than to test hypotheses, as in Chapter 3.

---

[1] All of the individuals in this book have been given pseudonyms to protect their privacy, and
some identifying details have been changed.

Interview Procedures

We interviewed students and their mothers, language arts teachers, and guidance counselors. The maternal interviews were completed in person at the student's home or over the telephone when students were in middle school. We tried to schedule these interviews during the students' sixth-grade school year, but some interviews occurred after the school year ended. We solicited information from mothers about their involvement in their children's schooling, their educational expectations for their children, challenges they faced regarding their children's progress in school, and general background demographics.

Interviews with students were conducted and audiotape recorded at the student's school and later transcribed. The protocol included both forced-response and open-ended questions related to literacy attitudes and practices, school experiences and achievement, and home life experiences related to literacy and achievement. Interviewers prompted students to elaborate on forced-response questions and facilitated detailed narratives in response to open-ended questions. Students also provided writing samples in response to a prompt. The content of student writing samples was analyzed. The seventh-grade writing prompt asked the students to speculate about where they would be 10 years later. The student interviews helped to provide a context for literacy variables, and the writing samples helped inform us about the students' level of motivation.

During the school visits, researchers interviewed the students' English teachers and guidance counselors, collecting details about each student's actual progress and behavior in school, the teachers' and counselors' expectations for the student's educational attainment, and reports of parental involvement. These practitioners also completed surveys about their classroom characteristics, their curriculum, and their work with the student, providing us with rich information about each child's classroom context.

Finally, researchers wrote up detailed field notes after their school and home visits, including information and impressions about the settings, attitude, and behavior of the participants throughout the interviews, noting anything unusual that may have occurred during the visit.

Measures

As described in Chapter 3, we continued to administer a battery of literacy assessments including vocabulary (PPVT-R) and comprehension (CAT). At each school visit, teachers were asked to state their expectations for the student's likely level of educational attainment on a 5-point scale from dropout (*1*) to graduate school (*5*). In their interviews, students were asked to report grades in core subject areas: language arts, math, science, and social studies. We were able to collect actual copies of report cards for some, but not all, students, and we used those to test for reliability of self-reports. Grades were converted to numbers, added, and divided by 4 to produce a standard grade point average, with a possible maximum of 4.0.

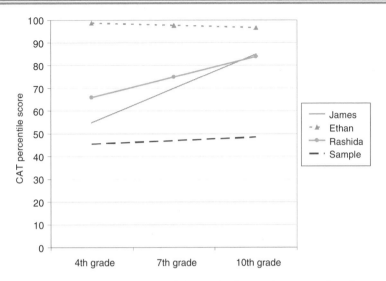

Figure 4.1. California Achievement Test (CAT; Searle, Casella, & McCulloch, 1992) reading comprehension percentile trajectories for focal children from elementary through high school.

Students Selected for Case Studies

Two White boys, James and Ethan, and one African American girl, Rashida, were selected from the 45 students who continued to participate in the study through the beginning of high school. These three students were chosen because they consistently scored above the group mean on standardized literacy measures. Their percentile scores on reading comprehension from Grades 4 though 10 are shown in Figure 4.1. Although Ethan scored consistently at ceiling, James and Rashida made gains. Reflecting these standardized indicators, the students' teachers throughout elementary school and into the beginning of middle school expected them to be highly successful in their paths to higher education (see Figure 4.2). Yet, these same students who did well in elementary school went on to do poorly in middle and high school. Perhaps not coincidentally, as we discuss in this chapter, they also all experienced serious disruptions at school during those years. Figure 4.3 shows the students' grade point averages in four core subjects (language arts, math, science, and social studies) for middle school (Grades 6 and 7) and high school (Grade 9), highlighting the strong contrast between ability (exemplified by reading comprehension assessments shown in Figure 4.1) and falling grades.

Group Analyses as a Backdrop for Case Studies

Cross-time correlations revealed that, although teacher expectations for the three students' educational attainment and reported grade point average in core subjects were both correlated with student ability as measured by scores on standardized tests through middle school, these relationships were no longer apparent as students entered high school (see Table 4.1). Once the students entered ninth

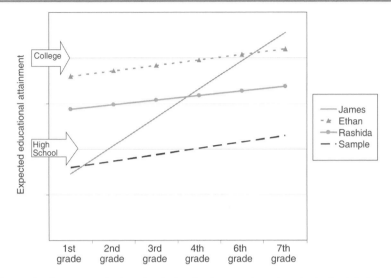

Figure 4.2.   Elementary school teachers' educational expectation trajectories for focal students.

grade, vocabulary and reading comprehension assessments were no longer correlated with grade point average.

In our analyses of middle and high school data for the whole group, we
found no relationship between literacy achievement, as measured by standardized
tests,[2] and school achievement, as measured by grade point average. Figure 4.4
shows a plot of reported grade point average against vocabulary scores at ninth
grade, with focal students highlighted.

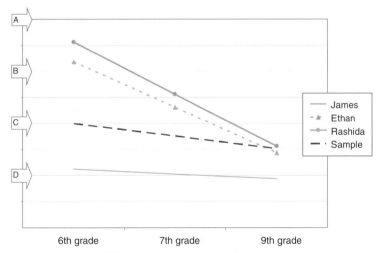

Figure 4.3.   GPA trajectories for focal students in middle school.

[2]The PPVT-R, the WRAT-R, and the reading subtest of the CAT.

Table 4.1. Correlations between standardized literacy assessments and academic progress markers

Academic success	4th-grade teacher rating of expected educational attainment	7th-grade teacher rating of expected educational attainment	6th-grade GPA	7th-grade GPA	9th-grade GPA
Literacy Assessments					
PPVT-R kindergarten	.43** (47)	.55*** (51)	.21 (50)	.33* (51)	−.05 (41)
4th-grade CAT-C	.42** (46)	.62*** (46)	.41** (49)	.20 (47)	.05 (39)
7th-grade CAT-C	.53*** (42)	.79*** (50)	.49*** (47)	.30* (51)	−.13 (40)
10th-grade CAT-C	.48** (30)	.61*** (37)	.60*** (37)	.52*** (38)	.06 (34)

$^*p < .05;\ ^{**}p < .01;\ ^{***}p < .001$

More surprising than the lack of relationship between grades and achievement as measured by standardized language and literacy assessments was the difficulty that these three students were having in school. These were students who consistently scored higher than all other participants in the Home–School Study on standardized tests and whom research staff, teachers, and parents all expected to sail through high school and into college. Yet, all three of them ended up having serious academic difficulties in high school.

Table 4.2 presents a conceptually clustered matrix highlighting themes such as academic self-esteem and gender role expectations across the lives of these three

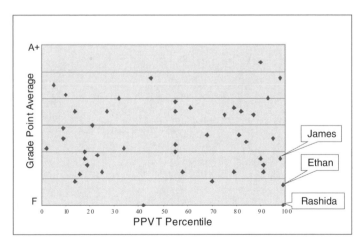

Figure 4.4. Ninth-grade grade point averages by PPVT-R percentile: Three students with high vocabulary scores who are at risk for school failure.

Table 4.2. Summaries of material collected on case-study students

Theme	James	Ethan	Rashida
	Preschool to elementary school		
Standardized assessment scores	High	High	High
Home Support for Literacy	High	High	High
School history	Moved from smaller suburban school setting to larger urban school	Attended high-performing urban K–8	Attended urban schools and for a short period was bused from urban neighborhood to suburban elementary school
	Middle school		
Academic factors	Consistent poor grades in middle school	Dramatic drop in grades in middle school	Dramatic drop in grades in middle school
Motivation	Demonstrated and expressed lack of motivation to succeed academically	Demonstrated motivation to pursue acting career but expressed little motivation for school	Enjoyed school and showed high motivation to attend college; was supported by mother and teachers
Academic self-esteem	Expressed high confidence	Expressed high confidence	Was modest in talking about academic self-worth but gave high ratings on self-report assessment of self-esteem
Family stressors and school disruptions	Experienced domestic violence in home and parental divorce; moved out of state	Moved from urban to suburban community; experienced death of grandmother	Experienced frequent moves, change in family constellation
Gender role expectations	Was taunted by father for being weak, engaged in serious fights at school	Exhibited need to prove masculinity and defend sexuality	Was responsible for caregiving for younger sisters
Supportive adults	Was close to mother, estranged from father	Was close to mother, combative with father	Had good relationship with mother, received rare visits with father, had good relationships with counselors at school
Peer relations	Described friends as intimidated by him	Harassed daily by peers	She had few close friends because of shyness and frequent moves

(continued)

Table 4.2. *(continued)*

Theme	James	Ethan	Rashida
	High school and beyond		
Status	Dropped out in 10th grade; demonstrated behavioral problems at school	Is on track to graduate from alternative high school	Had to repeat 9th grade because of lack of credits due to attendance
Future plans	GED	Has no higher education plans	Wants to attend college if she has financial support

students, showing comparisons between James, Ethan, and Rashida. It shows the kinds of middle school and early high school challenges all three students faced—challenges that apparently rendered their academic skills extraneous in determining their school success.

James: Acting Out/Dropping Out

James is an only child whose mother dropped out of school when she had him. She later received her general education diploma (GED) and subsequently completed some college courses. James's father married his mother a few years after James was born. Early on the family, although poor, was making ends meet, with both parents working. James was recognized by some of his early elementary school teachers as being a good student who liked to read, although he was less enthusiastic about writing activities. In his elementary school records, he was consistently rated as above average on all reading assessments. However, his primary teachers also noted that he was strong willed and could be difficult to manage sometimes. As one put it, "He wants to be an underachiever."

When James transitioned to middle school, his real academic trouble began. His mother attributed much of the blame to the structural differences between middle and elementary school.

His grades plummeted 'cause he was just trying to be, like, the class clown. Fooling around and talking to all the kids. They can get away with a lot more [in middle school].

James himself agreed that his grades were "pretty horrible," and explained that he could "find no reason to try." In his interviews, James complained about the move into a large middle school where he no longer received as much attention and perhaps encountered more competition. In his sixth-grade writing sample, he talked about a future in which he would go on to college but his friends would drop out of school.

Although still performing well academically, James began acting out. At first his actions could be described as merely mischievous, but later he engaged in much more serious acts, such as drinking and fighting, which resulted in his being suspended from school. This acting out strained his social relations; he told us, "The kids were definitely afraid of me but that didn't stop them" from being his friends.

He described being shunned at school mainly because school staff saw him as a troublemaker. This coincided with, and may well have been driven by, turbulent circumstances within the family; his father was charged with domestic violence and child abuse. James witnessed a great deal of violence in his home and expressed himself in violent ways at school. He became estranged from his father, although he remained close to his mother. He told us that his father blamed all of the family troubles, as well as James's school difficulties, on his mother. According to James, his father said she coddled him too much when he was younger. "And he's not willing to accept the blame for his own actions. My dad thinks I'm the root of all his problems," James added.

Whereas his mother talked about how independent James was for being able to be left alone to fend for himself, he described himself as isolated and closed off from others around him. In one interview he told us, "My voice and demeanor might be monotonous, but apparently I don't have any emotion that I like to show anyone."

In ninth grade, he was expelled from school on charges of sexual harassment. He declined to elaborate on the incident in interviews except to deny that he had really done anything wrong. After being expelled, he enrolled at another school but dropped out before finishing the 10th grade.

James attributed his problems in school to his "complete lack of motivation." He went on to say that, "In my German class, my teacher said literally I could pass the class with a blindfold and my arms behind my back. But I don't try." This rejection of school and lack of motivation can be understood as the sort of laddish self-protection/self-handicapping strategy, described by Jackson (2002) as one barrier to boys' academic achievement.

A Boy Named Sue: Homophobia, Bullying, and Fighting Back

Ethan consistently outscored all of the other participants in the study from the first standardized assessment given at age 5. He came from a highly literate home, with parents who were engaged in creative, albeit poorly paying, jobs. Although his mother had not completed high school, she was an avid reader who wrote poetry and short stories, and his father was a carpenter and amateur filmmaker. Ethan's parents provided strong support and encouragement for his early reading efforts and for his achievement in school.

Ethan had limited interactions with his older brother, who was almost 10 years his senior. As a teenager, the older boy had been sent off to live with his grandmother, and then later had ended up in and out of jail. Ethan spent his first 14 years living in a diverse urban neighborhood and attending a highly rated elementary school; however, the family was forced to move to a more conservative suburban setting. This was a turbulent move for the family, but necessary financially in that it gave them the opportunity to live in the house of a relative for much less money than they had been paying previously to rent an apartment. Thus, Ethan's early successes were shadowed by this move, which exacerbated his difficult transition to middle school and his journey through adolescence. Although he had once been a model student, he began to lose interest in academics. "I used to read a lot, and now I just have more stuff to do. You know, I've got a more complex life, I guess," he noted.

Furthermore, although Ethan acknowledged that the move was an opportunity for something new, it was precipitated by the loss of his grandmother. He admitted that he was going through a difficult grieving process:

When I was in [my old school], I was a bit depressed. I just wanted a fresh start and I found out, you know, it follows you no matter where you go. To be honest, I was just drinking. I don't know, I was depressed because my grandmother died. And that was the first time I had to deal with death.

This loss made Ethan vulnerable to being unmoored academically. His grades began to drop in seventh grade and his teachers commented on their concern about his lack of effort. When he began to miss assignments, came to class unprepared, and often arrived late, they reiterated that he was a "very bright" student who needed "to apply himself more."

Middle school students can be cruel, and Ethan experienced endless teasing because of his effeminate last name, *Sue.* "I've had to put up with this kind of shit all my life [because of my name]," he said. The teasing progressed to verbal and physical bullying in high school as Ethan began to explore his sexuality, or at least his open friendships with other students who were exploring their sexuality. "I get a lot of crap because of me being in the Gay–Straight Alliance. So people give me crap and call me faggot and, you know." The fact that he had a girlfriend in another city did little to deter the abuse he experienced at school.

In ninth grade, not long after the Columbine shootings, we interviewed Ethan, and he described in great detail how much pain he was in and how much he wanted to stop his tormentors.

I don't know. I just don't like the school because it's a bunch of like little rich, preppy bastards that get whatever they want in life and, you know, treat me like shit. I wish all the jocks would shut up. I really do. Just like those kids in Colorado. I know it's sick, but I really would like to see them all gone. I have fantasies about killing them sometimes.

Ethan found his teachers and counselors at school to be of no help, and he saw them as adversarial rather than supportive. Ethan's response to being called a "faggot" was to engage in hyper-masculine threats and revenge fantasies ("Just like those kids in Colorado. I know it's sick, but I really would like to see them all gone"), which he fortunately was able to distinguish from sincere intentions.

[The counselor is] always talking about how I'm going to end up dropping out of high school. Then she has the f**king audacity to say that I'm going to end up in prison with my brother because I might want to transfer. I swear I almost hit her in the face with a chair.

Ethan's progression through school was surprising to us because all of the researchers on the project, like his teachers through elementary school, pegged him as the most likely to excel in high school and go on to college. But in adolescence, academic concerns took a back seat to maintaining a masculine identity and to social problems in school and at home. Ethan named his brother as being someone he could trust and someone who knew him well: "He always sticks up for me and he always tells me, ya know, what to do and stuff like that." However, Ethan had very little contact with his brother and he told us, "I haven't seen him for the past 4 years . . . he don't want me to visit [him in jail] and I don't wanna visit there."

Although earlier home visits with Ethan provided indications that he had a good relationship with both his father and mother, he described a great deal of conflict with his father in his adolescent interviews:

[My dad] just comes home and sleeps like all f**king day. I never see him and then he just—like the first thing he'll ever say to me is usually just like yelling at me for something. I don't get any respect! It's like my birthday was yesterday, right, and I've got $115 in cash. You know what I did with that? I gave it all except the 20 bucks to my mom because they needed money until the next paycheck.

Rashida: Implications of a Lack of Social Capital

Rashida's mother was in 10th grade when she dropped out of school to give birth to the first of her six daughters. As the oldest, Rashida became increasingly responsible for caring for her younger siblings. The family moved often and was twice homeless during the course of their participation in the study. Rashida's mother had several long-term relationships with her children's fathers, but because she never married and had no other income to support her, she relied on what was then called Aid to Families with Dependent Children (AFDC; now called TANF) for assistance. However, Rashida's mother did get a GED and also completed a certificate course on early child care in preparation for working with young children. During a brief period when Rashida was in seventh grade, the household grew to include, in addition to her mother and siblings, her mother's boyfriend and three cousins. Once, in high school, Rashida moved back and forth between her mother and godmother's homes, although she remained in frequent contact with her mother and provided care for her younger sisters even when she wasn't living with them. These chaotic living conditions were exacerbated by the high crime rates in the neighborhood, described by Rashida in one of the writing exercises as a place where gangs and violence "isn't unusual" and where a friend was shot to death at a party. Throughout these various household constellations, Rashida had limited and inconsistent contact with her biological father.

Rashida's mother, because she was so young and had so few educational and financial resources, was unable to provide much support to Rashida's early literacy development. Our observations of Rashida with her mother when Rashida was 3 and 4 years old revealed a competitiveness more reminiscent of interactions with an older sibling than with a parent. The early reading activities her mother would involve her in were punitive rather than engaging, not unlike other interactions between the two. Thus, it is not surprising that Rashida became soft-spoken, reserved, polite, and eager to please. Nevertheless, she was a highly engaged reader in early childhood, and school was a place where teachers fostered her skills and interests.

Throughout elementary school, Rashida was well liked by her teachers and classmates, and she was highly praised. As her first-grade teacher noted, she was at "the top of her class" and "the best reader." In contrast, her mother's assessments varied and were less flattering. At an early visit in preschool, Rashida's mother predicted that Rashida would drop out of high school, just as she herself had done. Later, Rashida's mother did encourage her to complete high school and go to college, although she was unable to provide more than limited support for further education.

Beginning when Rashida was in second grade, she began to accumulate an alarming number of absences and was often tardy, and she continued this pattern throughout high school. In third grade, she missed almost 3 months of school when her family moved into a homeless shelter; however, she maintained a high level of reading skills. The following year, the family was homeless again for a month, and by the time Rashida entered middle school she and her family had moved eight times altogether. Rashida ended up repeating ninth grade because she was not in attendance enough to receive credit for her core classes. At various times her absentee rate was attributed to her mother's inability to get her to school (later indications suggested that Rashida was staying home to care for younger siblings) and to a series of illnesses. These absences were often unexcused because Rashida's mother failed to provide notes of explanation or letters from doctors.

Even as Rashida's teachers noted their frustration with her mother's poor record of maintaining contact with them and getting her daughter to school, they also acknowledged that Rashida always made up homework assignments promptly, neatly, and accurately. Rashida's mother was also successful in enrolling her in a suburban elementary school for a short time, which was superior to the one available in their urban neighborhood.

In contrast to the boys included in these case studies, Rashida managed to maintain some positive relationships with staff at the various schools she attended. Teachers at Rashida's middle school chose her to participate in a study group that was implemented in order to encourage promising students with limited resources to go on to college. In her 10th-grade writing sample, Rashida named a support staff member and her guidance counselor as two of the adults she could count on to discuss her problems. Unfortunately, she appeared to compartmentalize the ways in which these adults could help her make progress in school. On the one hand she expressed comfort in seeking them out for help with emotional issues, such as dealing with gang violence and subsequent loss; but on the other hand, she claimed to not know whom to turn to for assistance once she found out she was repeating ninth grade because of absences. Her mother reinforced this lack of agency, as evidenced by Rashida's comment, "She just keeps telling me to just try and do my work and hopefully they'll put me in the right grade."

DISCUSSION

James, Ethan, and Rashida all experienced educational and personal crises in middle school, and they had varying degrees of success in response to these crises. In the interviews, the boys both adopted attitudes of hegemonic masculinity, emphasizing their toughness, independence, willingness to fight, hypermasculine laddism (see Francis, 1999; Willis, 1977), and disdain for reading school assignments. Rashida's story told a different tale, however—one characterized by a chronic health problem, excessive absences due to family problems, and bewilderment about school bureaucracies and the path to higher education. Unfortunately, she also received little support from adults to help her navigate these challenges.

Results from these case studies echo findings from research literature on predictors of long-term academic success and from many sources that document the decline of achievement motivation, academic outcomes, socioemotional well-being, and academic orientation, during the period of adolescence (Garnier, Stein, & Jacobs, 1997). Many hypotheses have been offered to explain that decline (Battin-Pearson et al., 2000), and no doubt there is some truth to most of them. The phenomenon is widespread and almost certainly multiply determined. We present a more complete review of the relevant literature in Chapter 5. Here, we highlight the factors, for which some research evidence exists, that seem to be relevant in particular to the cases of James, Ethan, and Rashida.

Disengagement from School

Students might become less engaged in school in early adolescence for many reasons. School tasks become more challenging and less connected to their lives at precisely the point when students develop a wide array of nonacademic interests and when they have more autonomy about how they spend their time. Taking a life course perspective using data from a low-income sample, Alexander, Entwisle, and Horsey (1997) found patterns suggesting that disengagement occurs as early as first grade and paves the way for high school dropout. Good readers such as the three students we have focused on in this chapter might become bored in classrooms where low expectations and traditional teaching are the rule, or, such as Ethan, be unable to focus on their studies in environments they experience as hostile. Poor performance in classes often leads to decline of motivation (Roderick & Camburn, 1999), and poor academic performance in middle school is a strong predictor of high school dropout (Chevalier & Lanot, 2002; Thompson, 2002). The constraints of testing and curricular requirements may mean that students have decreasing interest in their school-related reading as they progress through school (McKenna, Kear, & Ellsworth, 1995; Moje, 2006; Porche & Ross, 2003; Porche, Ross, & Snow, 2004). Analysis of interviews of the Home–School study participants revealed a growing chasm in attitudes toward school texts versus the popular magazines and novels the students chose to read on their own in middle school (Ross, Roach, & Tabors, 2000).

Orientation Toward the Peer Culture

Harter (1993; Harter & Connell, 1984) has demonstrated that adolescents value competence in social and academic domains, as well as personal appearance, and suffer from low self-esteem if they feel inadequate in those domains. Adults, however, value academic competence and behavior regulation much more highly. Orientation to the peer culture can distract adolescents from academic achievement, in particular for students whose peer reference groups are not academically oriented.

Gender

Although a lot of talk in the popular press occurs about how boys lag behind girls in reading (Conlin, 2003), considerable overlap exists in early reading ability (Snow et al., 1998). However, the disparities between boys and girls in language arts become more pronounced in adolescence (Coley, 2001; Roderick, 2003). Some argue that these reflect biological factors (Gurian & Henley, 2001), though evidence is weak. More compelling are theories of the social construction of masculinity, which suggest that reading is identified with femininity (Askew & Ross, 1988; Kimmel, 2000) and that boys who chose to emphasize their masculine identities may thus actively avoid literacy activities and academic success

(Connell, 1995), as was the case with James and Ethan. Willis (1977) argued that boys from low-income backgrounds understand their limited opportunities for higher education and white-collar jobs and actively reject school culture as irrelevant to the labor positions they will soon hold, opting for "laddishness" rather than courting the chance of failure (Nayak, 2003). Poor performance and lack of engagement in school have been identified as a self-protective strategy (Martin, Marsh, & Debus, 2001) that is particularly prevalent for boys afraid of failing (Jackson, 2002). Though of course we can only speculate, a self-protective stance did seem to characterize both Ethan's and James's attitudes toward school.

Change in School Structures and Relationships with Adults

As students move from small elementary schools to much larger middle and high schools, and from spending most of the day with one teacher to having four or more teachers, they often lose the sense of connection to adults that supports an academic orientation. Adolescents may not locate a supportive adult in their large and chaotic secondary schools or, such as Ethan, may even experience those adults as uninterested or hostile. Eccles and colleagues (Eccles & Midgley, 1989; Eccles, et al, 1993; Eccles, Wigfield, & Schiefele, 1998) followed a large group of students through middle school and concluded that negative patterns in achievement were less an expected consequence of the early adolescent developmental period than a consequence of decline in teacher–student relations, reduced teacher efficacy, and increased ability tracking associated with the middle school environment (see also Chung, Elias, & Schneider, 1998).

Conversely, relational factors unavailable to James, Ethan, or Rashida have been identified as critical to academic achievement (Raider-Roth, 2005), especially as students enter adolescence. At-risk students who have good relationships with adults are more likely to achieve in middle school (Reed, McMillan, & McBee, 1995). Smaller schools that allow a varied curriculum and opportunities for strong positive relationships between students and teachers have lower dropout rates (Lee & Burkam, 2003). Adolescents who feel a sense of belonging to school have better psychological health and fewer school behavioral problems (Anderman, 2002).

SUMMARY

Multiple factors in adolescents' lives can derail a successful academic trajectory, and in fact, these factors appear to have a multiplicative rather than additive effect. Each of the students we focused on in our case studies lived in a family situation in which poverty was an underlying risk factor. Lack of housing resources led to frequent moves, a factor that is related to poorer school functioning (Nelson, Simoni, & Adelman, 1996). Each of these students described troubled relationships with parents, particularly with fathers. Much research on resiliency has shown the positive impact of supportive adults and effective parenting on children's socio-emotional and achievement outcomes (Masten, 2001; Masten et al., 1999). The poorer academic outcomes of the students highlighted in this chapter compared with those in the group who fared better has much to do with the availability of supportive adults in general, and strong parental support in particular.

These cases also highlight the ways that educators can be ineffective in promoting achievement, from instances in which these students fell through the cracks even with teachers' best intentions to provide accelerated learning to examples in which teachers failed to protect adolescents whose physical and psychological safety was in jeopardy from bullying or harassment (Stein, Tolman, Porche, & Spencer, 2002). In a study of a low-income, high-needs urban district, researchers found that even controlling for home influences on achievement, teacher quality (credentials, degrees, experience) was significantly related to student performance, and that teachers with higher qualifications gravitated to more affluent districts (Ascher & Fruchter, 2001). Furthermore, high-quality literacy instruction cannot be presumed; researchers have found that even exemplary teachers are inconsistent in their use of effective pedagogical practice (Bradford, 1999).

The message of the three case studies presented in this chapter reinforces our claims about continuity in literacy development; all three of the students profiled here started out in kindergarten well prepared to learn to read, and they excelled in reading at all ages, both on our assessments and in the eyes of their teachers. But excellent literacy skills are not enough to ensure success in school; motivation, engagement, effort, and orientation to the values and expectations of supportive adults are also necessary. Good readers who lack these other resources can end up as school failures and dropouts as surely as students with inadequate reading skills.

5

Motivational and Scholastic Resources that Predict Academic Success

The previous chapters present evidence found for low-income students in our longitudinal Home–School Study of Language and Literacy Development that has been previously documented several times (e.g., Walker, Greenwood, Hart, & Carta, 1994) with more heterogeneous groups: Early accomplishments in language and in literacy-related domains predict good performance in literacy throughout the school years. In short, early reading skills predict later reading skills, oral language and emergent literacy skills predict early reading skills, and difficulties in acquiring reading skills in first grade often presage persistent problems with reading achievement.

We also have documented the reassuring findings that many of the children in our group were performing quite well on our literacy assessments, even though we intentionally selected a group likely to include high-risk readers. The participants came from low-income families in which most of the parents had not gone beyond a high school diploma and some had even less education. The participants had, on average, attended preschool programs of only mediocre quality in their provision of language and literacy learning experiences, and they had mostly attended urban schools with poor to average school performance. Despite all of these risk factors, this group of children, in fourth grade, matched the national norming group on a standardized assessment of reading comprehension. Although a few of the children were showing frank learning disabilities and/or emotional problems that disrupted literacy learning, the vast majority of the participants in this study were functioning within one standard deviation of the population mean on normed literacy assessments, and a good proportion of the participants were well above the mean and well above grade level in their reading skills.

EXPANDING OUR DEFINITION OF ACADEMIC OUTCOMES

One of the goals of this study is to forge a link between definitions of academic outcomes typical of literacy researchers—reading at grade level, reading to learn, writing well, passing the language arts assessments reflecting state standards—and definitions more widely used in policy circles—progressing through the grades on time, not being identified for special services, avoiding contact with the juvenile justice system, graduating from high school, and entering tertiary education or the job market well prepared for any challenges. Although our group of children from low-income homes was normally distributed around the population mean on literacy measures, it was somewhat skewed toward the bottom end on the more policy-relevant factors.

Table 5.1 shows how this group fared on a variety of such factors. It can be seen that a rather high proportion of the participants in this group had been retained; had received special services; and were, as 10th graders, already identified as being unlikely to finish high school on time or at all. Although teen pregnancy is often cited as a risk factor, especially when compounded by poverty (Hao & Cherlin, 2004), we found it to be less salient in this group, in which pregnancy was not a clear precursor to school failure or disengagement. It is important to note that this group of students experienced the impact (for some at just the wrong time in their high school careers) of the newly introduced requirement that they pass a statewide assessment, in addition to fulfilling other requirements, in order to graduate. The Massachusetts Comprehensive Assessment System (MCAS) is a rather rigorous set of tests that was administered to 10th graders starting in 1998. In 2003, diplomas were denied for the first time to students who had not passed both the math and the language arts portions of this test (as happened for one student in our group). The impact of the high stakes associated with the MCAS on anticipatory dropout among students who had failed the test in 10th and 11th grades has been widely speculated about (Vaishnav, 2004); reports from participants in our study confirm its relevance.

Unfortunately, as the portraits of individual children presented in the previous chapter suggest, literacy skills do not translate automatically into academic success. We tend to think that children in the primary grades who do well in reading are doing well in general, and indeed that is usually the case—in primary school. But as children progress through elementary into middle and secondary school, the link between reading well and succeeding academically becomes much more tenuous. Of course, students who read poorly are unlikely to perform adequately in academically demanding courses, so poor reading skills do predict poor academic achievement with high reliability. But reading well is clearly not the only qualification for performing well later in the school years. The following questions guided the analyses to be presented in this chapter:

• What are the academic outcomes for participants in the Home–School Study after the primary grades? We wanted to know whether high-performing stu-

Table 5.1. Academic factors for the longitudinal sample

	Percent	n
Retention		
Early elementary	19%	9
Middle school	13%	6
High school	17%	8
Retained more than once between kindergarten and 12th grade	10%	5
Special services: Early elementary school		
Special Education	19%	9
Chapter 1[a]	25%	12
Special services: Middle school		
Special education	25%	13
Counseling	20%	10
Type of high school attended		
Public high school	73%	35
Vocational school	17%	8
Private school	10%	5
Secondary school/college status		
Has dropped out or plans to drop out	26%	12
Graduated high school or on track to graduate[b]	40%	19
Attending college or on track to attend college	34%	16
Teenage parent still in high school	2%	1
Teenage parent dropped out of high school	6%	3

[a]Services that were provided by Chapter 1 are now provided through Title 1.

[b]Includes one student who completed high school but did not pass the Massachusetts Comprehensive Assessment System (MCAS) examination, so the individual received a Certificate of Completion rather than a high school diploma.

dents in elementary school would continue to perform well into middle school and high school.

- How do academic outcomes relate to participants' literacy skills? Although we expected that there would be a correlation between academic outcomes and student scores on standardized literacy assessments, we also knew that it would not be perfect.

- What factors besides literacy skills predict long-term academic outcomes? We hypothesized that motivation would play a major role in students' academic success, controlling for literacy skills and ability.

In addition to the indicators of academic success or risk listed in Table 5.1, one might argue that affective aspects of students' lives are markers of academic accomplishment. Schools are, after all, not just designed to produce readers, or to produce graduates. Ideally they would produce eager learners, self-regulated and highly motivated individuals who are capable of planning their futures realistically and applying themselves to the new learning tasks that emerge. Ideally they would produce adults who are both curious and skeptical, interested in ongoing learning but capable of weighing the credibility of information presented to them. Ideally they would produce eager as well as competent readers, adults who read regularly to inform themselves and to expand their horizons. Ideally they would produce citizens who are respectful of authority but also ethically self-determining and resistant to the unfair exercise of authority. Of course, we don't have standardized measures of most of these ideal outcomes, but we did carry out extensive interviews with participants in the study, and we collected writing samples from them about their plans. These generated information about students' plans for the future and their goals and aspirations, as did the more traditional, standard assessments of motivation and engagement we administered.

MOTIVATION AND LEARNING

Motivation is an integral part of the learning process (Sivan, 1986), complementing the cognitive processes that we often think of as central. Motivation is inclusive and multifaceted; the construct embraces self-efficacy and competence beliefs (Wigfield & Eccles, 1992) and differentiates intrinsic origins (e.g., interest, curiosity, involvement) from extrinsic origins (e.g., recognition, grades) (Baker, Scher, & Mackler, 1997; Wigfield & Guthrie, 1997). Eccles and colleagues (1993) summarized motivation as the following two constructs: students' self-concept of ability and expectations for success ("Can I succeed on this task?") and students' goals for or valuing of achievement ("Do I want to succeed on this task").

Reading and Motivation

Many studies have shown that more engaged and motivated children become more proficient readers than do their counterparts who lack engagement and motivation in reading (Guthrie, Wigfield, & VonSecker, 2000; Snow, Barnes, Chandler, Hemphill, & Goodman, 1991; Sweet, Guthrie, & Ng, 1998). Good readers have been found to be highly motivated and to credit their success to effort rather than to have been found (Wigfield & Aster, 1984). Reading motivation has been highly correlated with reading amount, which in turn has been significantly correlated with reading comprehension, even after controlling for previous reading achievement, prior knowledge, and self-efficacy (Guthrie, Wigfield, Metsala, & Cox, 1999). Studies have shown that both extrinsic and intrinsic motivations are positively correlated with students' reading (Wigfield & Guthrie, 1997). Intrinsic motivation has been shown to be a better predictor of reading outcomes for elementary than for middle school students (Gottfried, 1990), but it predicts the amount and breadth of reading for middle school students (Guthrie et al., 1999; Wigfield, 1997). A positive relationship between intrinsic motivation and academic achievement has been observed for secondary school students across gender and ethnicity (Gottfried, 1982, 1985; Harter & Connell, 1984; Lloyd & Barenblatt, 1984).

It has also been shown that children's intrinsic motivation tends to decline during the elementary school years (Harter, 1981; Wigfield & Guthrie, 1997). Furthermore, students' engagement and motivation is not independent of their earlier success in reading acquisition, which in turn is influenced by children's emergent literacy skills or school readiness (Vellutino, 2003). Therefore, those who struggle with reading in early stages are more likely to be disengaged from reading activities in later grades, as predicted by the Matthew effect (Stanovich, 1986).

Gender and Motivation

Girls in elementary schools were found to have more positive motivation for reading than do boys in fourth and fifth grade (Wigfield & Guthrie, 1997) and fifth and sixth grade (Baker & Wigfield, 1999). Girls scored higher than did boys on many specific components of reading motivation, including self-efficacy (Wigfield & Guthrie, 1997) and involvement and compliance (Baker & Wigfield, 1999). Moreover, the relationship between reading motivation and reading achievement was stronger for girls. However, girls showed a more severe decline in motivation as a consequence of the middle school transition as compared with boys (Simmons & Blyth, 1987), although this depended on the school context. Specifically, girls who remained in elementary and middle school did not exhibit a decline in self-esteem; their advantage lasted even after their high school entry.

Socioeconomic Status, Ethnicity, and Motivation

In their study of 371 fifth and sixth graders in elementary school, Baker and Wigfield (1999) reported that mean scores of different reading dimensions were similar for students from low-income and middle-income families. Furthermore, African American students reported stronger motivation for reading than students of other ethnicities. However, the relationship between reading motivation and reading achievement was stronger for White students.

School Environments and Motivation

Anderman, Maehr, and Midgley (1999) attested the importance of school environment factors in concert with student needs and proved that negative shifts in motivation in middle schools are not inevitable. Of several school environmental factors, they focused on the concept of goals, which can be categorized into "task-focused goals" and "ability-focused goals" (Maehr & Anderman, 1993). Students with task-focused goals pursue learning for the sake of learning. In contrast, students with ability-focused goals pursue learning in order to demonstrate their ability. Maehr and Anderman (1993) argued that, at the school level, different goal sets are promoted by instructional practices. They related these instructional practices to "school cultures," and demonstrated how school culture relates to student motivation (Anderman et al., 1999). Specifically, students who transitioned to middle schools that employed more task-oriented instructional practices had less deterioration in motivation than students who moved to middle schools that employed competitive, ability-differentiating instructional practices. Task-oriented instruction promotes grouping students according to their interest rather than their ability. The task orientation leads students to focus on mastering tasks and learning. It was also shown that students and teachers in elementary school put more emphasis on task goals (Midgley, Anderman, & Hicks, 1995) than do middle school teachers.

Instruction and Motivation

Intrinsic motivation can be enhanced through the instructional approach employed. Guthrie and his colleagues (Guthrie et al., 1996; Guthrie et al., 2000) demonstrated that students who participated in a reading instruction they devised (Concept-Oriented Reading Instruction [CORI]) had higher intrinsic motivation. A central focus of the CORI intervention is building student motivation by including hands-on experiences, providing a variety of texts relevant to the topic so that students have a choice in what to read, and providing texts at the students' reading levels to reduce frustration.

In other studies, emphasis on student discipline and control was shown to influence student motivation. Elementary school teachers' beliefs differed from middle school teachers' beliefs on discipline, control, and efficacy (Eccles et al., 1993). Significantly more sixth- and seventh-grade teachers emphasized the importance of student discipline and control, and seventh-grade teachers felt less efficacious. Teachers' perceptions of students' intrinsic motivation and reading achievement were positively, significantly correlated (Gottfried, 1985; Sweet et al., 1998). Teachers tended to report that high achievers are intrinsically motivated while low achievers are extrinsically motivated (Sweet et al., 1998).

THE IMPORTANCE OF MIDDLE SCHOOL

There is considerable evidence (Anderman & Midgley, 1998; Roeser & Eccles, 1998; Roeser, Eccles, & Sameroff, 2000; Wigfield, Eccles, Mac Iver, Reuman, & Midgley, 1991) that long-term academic trajectories—the choice to stay in school or to drop out and the selection in high school of academic, college-prep courses versus basic level courses—are strongly influenced by experience in Grades 6–8. Many studies have shown that students' motivation declines from elementary school to middle school. A longitudinal study (Wigfield et al., 1991) followed 2,500 students from elementary school to middle school. Measures of students' beliefs and attitudes showed that students' self-esteem was lowest immediately after transition to middle school. Furthermore, students' estimates of their ability in English and social activities showed a marked decline after the transition to middle school. Another study (Eccles et al., 1983) confirmed that the largest differences in students' attitudes emerged at the transition from elementary school to middle school. Students' estimates of their own ability in mathematics and English were lower in the middle school years than in elementary or high school. Transition to middle school seems to be particularly debilitating for adolescents with learning disabilities, as the transition exacerbates achievement gaps between them and their peers without learning disabilities (Anderman, 1998). The achievement gap in math and science between students with and without learning disabilities was drastically reduced when adolescents with learning disabilities did not experience transition to middle school until ninth grade, even after controlling for gender, grades, ethnicity, perceptions of the quality of teaching, and socioeconomic status.

Some speculate on the reasons for this deterioration in motivation. Simmons and Blyth (1987) suggested that the decline in motivation is attributed to pubertal and school change. The students who face these two at the same time are more vulnerable. For example, girls are at a greater risk than boys because girls typically reach puberty earlier than boys. However, Nottelman's (1987) results showed that students who experienced the transition had higher self-esteem than those who did not. Other researchers focus on a match between students' developmental needs and environmental factors (i.e., competitive school environment; Eccles & Midgley, 1989). A poor fit between students' developmental needs and school environments may result in negative consequences for motivation. This line of thought and research investigates systematic differences in typical classroom and school environments between elementary and middle schools as a contributing factor to the decline in motivation. On the school and classroom side, traditional middle schools are characterized by larger class sizes and fewer opportunities for personal interactions between students and teachers. Teachers are usually subject-matter specialists and teach a large number of students. Traditional middle school classrooms are marked by more emphasis on teacher control and discipline and reduced opportunities for student decision making and self-management (Eccles et al., 1993). On the student side, adolescence is marked by increased desire for autonomy and social acceptance, more of a focus on identity issues and peer relationships, and advanced cognitive engagement in abstract thinking (Eccles et al., 1993). The mismatches between adolescents' developmental needs and traditional school environments include the following:

- Middle schools typically emphasize competition and social comparison during a period of adolescents' heightened focus on self.

- Fewer decision-making opportunities exist for adolescents during a period of increasing desire for autonomy.

- Fewer opportunities exist for adolescents to develop close personal relationships with teachers during a period when adolescents may need extra support from adults.

Experiences in Grades 6–8 are widely varied, in part, because the organization of schooling in these grades differs. Some districts have schools that house students from kindergarten through eighth grade (K–8 schools), with the major and only transition at ninth grade. In these K–8 schools, students in sixth through eighth grade typically have specialist teachers and a high school-like schedule of moving around from class to class, but the students remain in a relatively small and familiar school with teachers who know them and each other, and the sixth through eighth graders have the advantage of being the elders within the student population. Other districts have established middle schools to serve sixth through eighth graders in buildings intermediate in size between elementary schools and secondary buildings, and some districts have junior high schools that serve seventh through ninth graders. Both of these systems require that 12- to 14-year-olds make a transition to a new building, new classmates, and an unfamiliar set of teachers while at the same time transitioning to a new daily schedule and to being the "little kids" in the building. The middle school model, in principle, gives students access to better prepared specialist teachers for math, science, social studies, and language arts, but it also creates an isolated student body of immature adolescents all experiencing puberty, novel responsibilities, and novel risks during a relatively disorganized period of human development.

Of the students we followed into the middle grades, 46% entered a new school in sixth grade, 41% entered a new school in seventh grade, and the remainder (13%) transitioned in ninth grade (including those students who had already made a previous middle grade transition). Students attended different school settings. Many of our sixth-grade participants (57%) attended middle schools educating some configuration of fifth through eighth graders, while 19% attended schools educating students in kindergarten through eighth grade, and 21% attended schools educating students in kindergarten through sixth grade; the remainder of students attended special education settings. Because there was a relatively small number of students in each type of setting, we cannot make strong claims about the impact of school organization on academic trajectories; however, it is noteworthy that students who transitioned to middle school in sixth grade had low engagement in school and had low teacher ratings of their work habits; these students were at greater risk of doing poorly in school, as evidenced by their grades, than students who did not transition to middle school until seventh grade (Ross, Roach, & Tabors, 2000).

Given these various indicators that experiences in the middle grades are both highly varied and related to longer-term academic trajectories, we explore more deeply in the next section how these students felt about themselves as middle schoolers, what motivated them academically, and what scholastic resources they had available as they made the difficult transition into secondary school.

ASSESSING MOTIVATIONAL RESOURCES IN MIDDLE SCHOOL

We collected information in standardized ways about the participants' motivation, particularly in the middle school years. In fact, we see motivation as more than an outcome; motivational and affective commitments may be considered a resource to students as they progress through school and as they balance increasingly complex academic challenges along with the challenges of getting through adolescence. Motivational outcomes—engagement in school and school learning, a sense that one is competent as a learner, a sense that social support is available, a sense of being in control of one's life, the capacity for self-regulation, and expectations for one's future educational success—are crucial in keeping learners focused on school at a period in their lives when many find it irrelevant, boring, or unrewarding. School engagement, possibly key in explaining variation in achievement (Fredricks, Blumenfeld, & Paris, 2004), is a multifaceted construct because students can be engaged differentially in behavioral, emotional, and cognitive aspects of learning in educational contexts. In other words, students' achievement can be explained by the degree of engagement or disengagement in academic, social, and extracurricular activities; by positive and negative affect toward teachers and school; and by investment in cognitive challenges. Furthermore, young adolescents from low-income families who are attending urban schools may be more dependent on their own motivational resources than students from middle-income families, whose parents' focus on their academic success often constrains options such as missing classes, working many hours out of school, or dropping out.

Accordingly, we go beyond the external indicators of progress in Table 5.1 to report on the internal motivational resources available to the participants in this study. We collected data on 57 students in sixth grade and 54 students in seventh grade. In the next section we report on intermediate indicators of general scholastic success—the students' achievement on our literacy tests, the students' grades, and their teachers' evaluations of them as learners. The question that motivated us in both of these analyses was this: What motivational and scholastic resources do these middle school students have?

The middle-school participants are, of course, the group of students who were still participating in the study 10 and 11 years after the original data collection period during which they were 3 years old. During the interim, the group was reduced in size from the original 83 to 54. However, as shown in Table 2.1 in Chapter 2, the composition of the middle-school participants is consistent with the original group, and there were no significant differences between time periods for any of the demographic or language assessment variables. Thus, we conclude this middle school group is equivalent to the preschool group on these variables.

In order to gauge the types of motivational resources available to the students in middle school, interviews were conducted one-on-one with the students

Table 5.2. Sample assessment items reflecting motivational resources related to students' perceptions of competence, self-regulation, sources of support, engagement in school, and scholastic coping strategies

Instrument used for indicating student's motivational resources	Sample assessment items
Self-Perception Profile for Children (Harter, 1985a)	Some teenagers feel that they are just as smart as others their age BUT other teenagers are not so sure and wonder if they are as smart. Some teenagers are pretty slow to finish their work BUT other teenagers can do their work more quickly.
Rochester Assessment Package for Schools: Engagement Scale (RAPS-E; Connell, 1996)	When I'm in class, I try very hard. When I'm in class, I just act as if I'm working.
Social Support Scale for Children (Harter, 1985b)	Some kids have parents who don't really understand them BUT other kids have parents who really do understand them. Some kids don't have a teacher who helps them to do their very best BUT other kids do have a teacher who helps them to do their very best.
Self-Regulation Scale (Ryan & Connell, 1989)	I do my homework because I'll get in trouble if I don't. I do my classwork because I want to learn new things.
Multidimensional Measure of Children's Perceptions of Control (Connell, 1985)	When something bad happens to me in school (like not doing well on a test or not being able to answer an important question), • I tell myself it wasn't important. • I try to see what I did wrong.

as part of the assessment session. Embedded in the interviews were instruments chosen to indicate the students' perceived competence, self-regulation, sources of support, engagement in school, and scholastic coping strategies. Sample items reflecting each of these constructs are presented in Table 5.2.

When the children were in sixth grade, we administered a partial set of scales related to self-perception and engagement: the Harter Self-Perception Profile for Children (SPPC; Harter, 1985a) and the Rochester Assessment Package for Schools: Engagement Scale (RAPS-E; Connell, 1996). During the children's seventh-grade year we administered these two scales again (using the short form of the SPPC) and added the Social Support Scale for Children (SS; Harter, 1985b), the Rochester Assessment Package for Schools: Coping Scale (RAPS-C; Connell, 1996), the Self-Regulation Scale (SR; Ryan & Connell, 1989), and the Multidimensional Measure of Children's Perceptions of Control (PC; Connell, 1985). All scales administered were scored on a 4-point scale, with higher scores

Table 5.3. Descriptive statistics for motivational variables in 6th grade ($N = 57$)

Scale type	Variable	Mean	SD	Range	Norming mean	Norming SD
Self-perception[a]	Scholastic Competence	2.68	0.57	1.50–3.83	2.94	0.65
	Social Acceptance	3.07	0.64	1.67–4.00	2.95	0.68
	Athletic Competence	2.71	0.87	1.00–4.00	2.84	0.70
	Physical Appearance	2.74	0.90	1.00–4.00	2.78	0.69
	Behavioral Conduct	2.81	0.64	1.17–3.83	3.00	0.57
	Global Self-Worth	3.13	0.69	1.17–4.00	3.09	0.63
Engagement[b]	Total	3.09	0.39	2.24–3.77		

Note: Each of these scales is scored on a 4-point scale and then an average is taken based on the number of questions answered.

[a]Harter Self-Perception Profile for Children (Harter, 1985a). Norming means and standard deviations from *Manual for Self-Perception Profile of Children* (Harter, 1985a).

[b]Rochester Assessment Package for Schools: Engagement Scale (RAPS-E; Connell, 1996).

indicating greater agreement. Tables 5.3 and 5.4 present the descriptive statistics on each of these scales for sixth and seventh graders, respectively.

The sixth-grade results show that, on average, the students perceived themselves to be doing best in terms of Global Self-Worth (3.13) and least well in terms of Scholastic Competence (2.68), although they reported that their Total Engagement in school was, on average, quite high (3.09). By seventh grade, however, students' perceptions of their Global Self-Worth, Scholastic Competence, and Total Engagement had all decreased. The students, on average, felt most supported by friends and parents. They displayed Positive Academic Coping (3.35) and believed that their Effort (3.76) was what provided them with locus of control over their academic lives.

For seventh grade, the range of measures of motivational resources was more extensive and a bit more complex. The measures included subscales of the SPPC, RAPS, SR, and Locus of Control. When the 19 subscale scores were combined into a single composite, the alpha level was only .64, indicating a relatively low level of association among this large number of items. Because of this result and because we posited the existence of multidimensionality among these motivational variables, we performed a principal components analysis (PCA) with the full group of variables. Initial results from this multivariate analysis suggested that the measures did indeed divide into two primary components: 1) self-motivation and initiative to achieve in school, global feelings of self-worth, and support from adults and peers; and 2) an anxious response to outward influences (parents and

Table 5.4. Descriptive statistics for motivational variables in 7th grade ($N = 54$)

Scale type	Variable	Mean	SD	Range	Norming mean	Norming SD
Self-perception	Scholastic Competence	2.64	0.71	1.17–4.00	2.84	0.58
	Global Self-worth	3.03	0.76	1.50–4.00	3.10	0.55
Social support	Classmate	3.26	0.58	1.00–4.00	3.12	0.57
	Friend	3.54	0.54	1.50–4.00	3.25	0.67
	Parent	3.34	0.76	1.17–4.00	3.41	0.64
	Teacher	3.25	0.61	1.50–4.00	3.12	0.69
Engagement	Total	2.83	0.50	1.48–3.96		
Academic coping	Anxiety	2.12	0.85	1.00–4.00		
	Denial	2.27	0.79	1.00–4.00		
	Positive	3.35	0.61	2.00–4.00		
	Projection	1.78	0.72	1.00–4.00		
Self-regulation	External	3.19	0.67	1.33–4.00	2.77	0.74
	Identified	3.16	0.62	1.00–4.00	3.53	0.50
	Intrinsic	2.38	0.76	1.00–4.00	2.84	0.82
	Introjected	2.45	0.77	1.00–4.00	2.62	0.78
Locus of control	Control	3.25	0.62	2.00–4.00		
	Effort	3.76	0.51	2.00–4.00		
	Powerful others	2.10	0.67	1.00–3.50		
	Unknown	2.34	.98	1.00–4.00		

Note: Norming means and standard deviations for self-perception are from *Manual for Self-Perception Profile of Children* (Harter, 1985a); norming means and standard deviations for social support are from *Manual for Social Support Scale for Children* (Harter, 1985b); norming means and standard deviations for self-regulation are taken from Patrick, Skinner, and Connell (1993), based on Grades 3, 4, and 5. Each of these scales is scored on a 4-point scale and then an average is taken based on the number of questions answered.

teachers) and pressures to achieve, a tendency to blame others for scholastic failures, and a feeling of not knowing how to exert control over academic life.

Although alpha scores for variables grouped into these two dimensions were relatively high (.78 and .70, respectively), the eigenvalues showed that less than 40% of the original variance would be accounted for in these large composites. Therefore, using PCA to further investigate the multidimensionality of these groups of motivational variables, we interpreted three dimensions for the first primary composite and two dimensions for the second primary composite. A summary of the five composites with their eigenvalues is given in Table 5.5.

The five dimensions of motivation can be subdivided into three positive and two negative dimensions. We characterized the positive dimensions as 1) Confident: reflecting strong feelings of self-worth globally and scholastically, as well as a perception of strong teacher support; 2) Determined: reflecting positive academic coping strategies and effort along with strong feelings of parental and

Table 5.5. Motivational resource composites

Rank of primary composite	Description	Eigenvalue
First primary composite	12 variables	3.74
Confident	Harter: Scholastic Competence, Global Self-Worth, Teacher Social Support	1.70
Determined	Harter: Parent and Friendship Social Support, Positive Academic Coping, Locus of Control: Effort	1.64
Self-regulatory	Total engagement, Harter Classmate Support, Identified and Intrinsic Self-Regulation, Locus of Control: Control	2.42
Second primary composite	7 variables	2.56
Anxious	Anxiety Academic Coping, External and Introjected Self-Regulation	1.80
Deflecting	Projection and Denial Coping, Powerful Others, Unknown Locus of Control	1.88

peer support; and 3) Self-Regulatory: reflecting strong engagement in general, intrinsic self-regulation and control over academic life, as well as strong feelings of support from classmates. We characterized the negative dimensions as 1) Anxious: reflecting anxiety-driven academic coping in response to the perceived authority of parents and teachers, and 2) Deflecting: blaming others for failure and relinquishing control.

In testing correlations among the seventh-grade motivational resource composites (Table 5.6), we found that three of the composites—Confident, Determined, and Self-Regulatory—were positively correlated, as were the composites for Deflecting and Anxious Motivation. Furthermore, there was a negative correlation between being confident and being anxious and deflecting. These findings seem to indicate that there are, indeed, two primary dimensions of motivational composites—a positive and a negative dimension—and that the students could reliably report their attitudes on these measures.

Subgroup analyses using the five dimensions of motivational resources revealed large subgroup differences on the Determined dimension. Students who had never experienced either retention or any special services tended to have lower

Table 5.6. Correlations among 7th-grade motivational resources composites ($N = 54$)

	Confident	Determined	Self-regulatory	Anxious	Deflecting
Confident	1.0				
Determined	0.49***	1.0			
Self-Regulatory	0.39**	0.43**	1.0		
Anxious	−0.34*	0.06	0.09	1.0	
Deflecting	−0.31*	−0.18	−0.09	0.37**	1.0

*$p < .05$; **$p < .01$; ***$p < .001$.

scores on this composite measuring parental and friendship support, positive academic coping, and effort ($t(54) = 1.96$, $p < .06$). In contrast, students who had received Chapter 1 services tended to have higher scores on this same dimension ($t(54) = -2.43$, $p < .02$). Perhaps students who received extra help reported feeling more supported by adults and peers than students who did not receive extra services, and this may have translated into the use of more coping strategies and putting more effort into school.

ASSESSING SCHOLASTIC RESOURCES IN MIDDLE SCHOOL

Scholastic resources in sixth and seventh grade were measured in three ways. First, we looked at actual performance on formal assessments of achievement such as those reported on in Chapter 3, as these constitute one important indicator of scholastic resources. We assessed the students' achievement levels with a battery designed to reflect a number of constructs: vocabulary knowledge using the Peabody Picture Vocabulary Test–Revised (PPVT-R; Dunn & Dunn, 1981), reading comprehension using the Analytical Reading Inventory (ARI; Woods & Moe, 1989) in sixth grade and the California Achievement Test (CAT; Searle et al., 1992) in seventh grade, word recognition using the Wide Range Achievement Test-Revised (WRAT-R: Reading; Jastak & Wilkinson, 1984) in sixth and seventh grades, arithmetic skills in seventh grade WRAT-R: Math (Jastak & Wilkinson, 1984), writing ability using an elicited essay on an assigned topic in sixth and seventh grade, and academic language asking for definitions of 10 basic words in sixth and seventh grade. Many of these were standardized assessments with extensive track records as reliable and valid measures. The writing and academic language assessments were nonstandardized measures that we developed to reflect a wider variety of skills. Ultimately, we formed a composite of some of these test scores to use in further analyses.

Second, we used student-reported grades in academic subjects to reflect the students' performance in school. Grades were converted to a 12-point scale (*12 = A+* to *0 = F*) and a grade average was developed for each student using grades in English/language arts, math, science, and social studies. Although one would expect grades to correlate highly with the composite score on academically oriented tests, grades are also influenced by other factors, such as the difficulty of the courses, evidence of student effort, and teacher attitude toward the student. Thus, although grades may be considered a less "pure" reflection of scholastic competence, they are a more ecologically valid measure—the measure that is taken into account for promotion to the next grade, for tracking, and for college admissions.

The third measure of scholastic resources was teacher ratings of the students participating in the study. The English or language arts teachers filled out the The Teacher–Child Rating Scale (T-CRS; Hightower et al., 1986), which is a one-page standardized questionnaire consisting of 38 questions divided into two parts. Part 1 consists of 18 behaviorally oriented items describing school problems. Teachers rated an individual student's behavior on a 5-point scale (from *not a problem* to *very serious problem*). These 18 items form three subscales: acting out (reflecting student problems of disruptiveness, impulsivity, and aggressiveness [e.g., *disruptive in class*]), shyness/anxiety (reflecting shy, withdrawn, and dependent behaviors [e.g., *anxious, worried*]), and learning skills (reflecting problems in skills needed to succeed in the school environment [e.g., *poorly motivated to achieve*]). Part 2 consists of 20 items assessing a student's strengths. Teachers noted their level of agreement with each of several positively worded statements (e.g. *completes work*) with reference to the target student. Again, each statement was on a 5-point scale. Four subscales were formed from the 20 items: frustration tolerance (reflecting a student's skills in tolerating and adapting to limits imposed by the school environment [e.g., *accepts imposed limits*]), assertive social skills (reflecting a student's interpersonal functioning and skills/confidence during interactions with peers [e.g., *comfortable as a leader*]), task orientation (reflecting a student's functional effectiveness within the educational setting [e.g., *works well without adult support*], and peer social skills (reflecting a student's likeability to peers [e.g., *makes friends easily*]). Teacher ratings can be transformed into a percentile (0–100) using the norms of the T-CRS. In every case, a higher percentile means the student exhibited better behavior/fewer problems. In subsequent analyses, the Teacher Rating of the Student's Learning Skills is the variable that was used.

Descriptive statistics on all of the sixth- and seventh-grade measures of scholastic resources can be found in the Tables 5.7 and 5.8, respectively. Again, it is worth noting that this group of students replicated the population distribution on the standardized tests quite closely, with mean scores within a few points of the norming mean of 100 on most measures, and average scores on the T-CRS close to the 50th percentile. In sixth grade, the reported grades for the group averaged a B-, while in seventh grade, the reported grades were approximately a C+. In other words, although these were children from low-income families who were attending generally average or below-average schools, they were not *as a group* failing to meet expected levels of academic achievement.

The measures of scholastic resources showed fairly high correlations with each other, both within grade across measures (Tables 5.9 and 5.10) and across grades within construct (Table 5.11). It is interesting to note that in sixth grade the PPVT-R, WRAT-R: Reading, and ARI were moderately correlated with Grade Average. However, none of these measures was correlated with Grade Average in seventh grade. It is not clear what would account for this change between sixth and seventh grade. We know that students' grades dropped slightly, on average, from sixth to seventh grade, so perhaps this was a contributing factor.

Given these strong correlations across the various measures within grade, and given the focus of the study, a composite was constructed reflecting literacy achievement for each student at each grade. The achievement indicators chosen for inclusion in the Literacy Composite were PPVT-R standard score, the WRAT-R: Reading standard score, and the Writing total score for both years. In addition, the ARI total score was included in the Literacy Composite for sixth grade, and the CAT percentile score was included in the Literacy Composite for seventh grade.

Table 5.7. Descriptive statistics for results of measures of scholastic resources in 6th grade

Variable	N	Norming mean	Mean	Norming SD	SD	Range
Achievement measures						
PPVT-R[a] standard score	57	100	97.95	15	15.59	69–141
WRAT-R[b] standard score	57	100	97.95	15	17.54	53–139
ARI[c] narrative Grade 3	57		12.25		3.00	1–16
Narrative Grade 5	57		12.88		2.71	4–16
Expository Grade 3	57		11.32		3.90	2–16
Expository Grade 5	57		9.84		3.52	0–15
Total score	57		45.28		10.55	12–62
Writing task form score	57		3.19		1.04	1–5
Content score	57		3.12		1.21	1–5
Total score	57		6.32		2.02	2–10
Academic language	56		6.83		2.02	0–10.6
Student-reported grades						
English	54		7.31		3.10	0–12
Math	52		7.21		2.82	2–11
Social Studies	53		7.02		3.19	0–11
Science	52		6.83		2.65	1–12
Grade Average	54		7.09		2.35	0.75–11
T-CRS[d]						
Not acting out	55	50	58.73		36.48	3–99
Not shy/anxious	55	50	52.00		34.34	1–99
Learning skills	55	50	39.38		29.82	1–99
Frustration tolerance	55	50	43.00		27.11	1–99
Assertive social skills	55	50	42.22		29.78	1–99
Task orientation	55	50	34.47		27.25	1–99
Peer social skills	55	50	41.24		29.80	2–99

[a]Peabody Picture Vocabulary Test–Revised (Dunn & Dunn, 1981).
[b]Wide Range Achievement Test–Revised (Jastak & Wilkinson, 1984).
[c]Analytical Reading Inventory (Woods & Moe, 1989).
[d]The Teacher–Child Rating Scale (Hightower et al., 1986).

Grade Average for sixth and seventh grade has been maintained as a separate indicator of scholastic resources, as has the Teacher Rating of Student's Learning Skills.

Perhaps the most striking fact about the Literacy Composite is its stability across sixth and seventh grade. Table 5.12 shows that, although the measures that went into the composites were taken a year apart and a different reading comprehension test was used each year, the correlation between the two composites is .90. The abilities that the students were able to demonstrate on these assessments remained highly consistent. Subgroup analyses using the sixth- and seventh-grade Literacy Composite showed that students who did not receive any special services scored significantly higher on the composite in both sixth and seventh grade than

Table 5.8. Descriptive statistics for results of measures of scholastic resources in 7th grade

Variable	N	Norming mean	Mean	Norming SD	SD	Possible range	Range
Achievement measures							
PPVT-R[a]: standard score	54	100	101.89	15	15.91		66–141
WRAT-R[b]: Reading standard score	54	100	98.00	15	15.07		61–138
WRAT-R: Math standard score	54	100	90.46	15	17.33		55–120
CAT[c] scale score	54		739.26		35.94	1–999	639–824
Percentile	54	50	51.19		25.2	1–100	2–98
Writing form score	53		3.36		0.98		1–5
Content score	53		3.62		0.95		1–5
Total score	53		6.98		1.74		2–10
Academic language	52		6.80		1.95		0.50–10.8
Student-reported grades							
English	52		6.69		2.85		0–11
Math	53		6.13		3.43		0–12
Social Studies	52		5.56		2.97		0–11
Science	53		6.32		3.53		0–12
Grade average	53		6.16		2.49		0.75–11
T-CRS[d]							
Not acting out	47	50	54.02		36.82		2–99
Not shy/anxious	47	50	55.96		33.72		1–99
Learning skills	47	50	40.51		30.56		2–99
Frustration tolerance	47	50	41.60		27.41		3–99
Assertive social skills	47	50	38.98		27.25		1–99
Task orientation	47	50	38.23		27.02		1–99
Peer social skills	47	50	44.32		30.11		1–99

[a]Peabody Picture Vocabulary Test–Revised (Dunn & Dunn, 1981).
[b]Wide Range Achievement Test–Revised (Jastak & Wilkinson, 1984).
[c]California Achievement Test (Searle et al., 1992).
[d]The Teacher–Child Rating Scale (Hightower et al., 1986).

Table 5.9. Correlations among 6th-grade measures of scholastic resources

	PPVT-R (n)	WRAT-R (n)	ARI: T (n)	Writing: Form (n)	Writing: Content (n)	Writing: Total (n)	Grade Average (n)	Teacher Rating (n)
PPVT-R[a]	1.0							
WRAT-R[b]	.64*** (57)	1.0						
ARI: T	.69*** (57)	.70*** (57)	1.0					
Writing: Form	.34** (57)	.49*** (57)	.41** (57)	1.0				
Writing: Content	.40** (57)	.36** (57)	.39** (57)	.60*** (57)	1.0			
Writing: Total	.42*** (57)	.47*** (57)	.45*** (57)	.88*** (57)	.91*** (57)	1.0		
Grade Average	.39* (54)	.34** (54)	.31* (54)	.12 (54)	.05 (54)	.10 (54)	1.0	
Teacher Rating	.43*** (55)	.32* (55)	.33* (55)	.15 (55)	.13 (55)	.15 (55)	.61*** (52)	1.0

*$p < .05$; **$p < .01$; ***$p < .001$.
[a]Peabody Picture Vocabulary Test–Revised (Dunn & Dunn, 1981).
[b]Wide Range Achievement Test–Revised (Jastak & Wilkinson, 1984).

Table 5.10. Correlations among 7th grade measures of scholastic resources

	PPVT-R (n)	WRAT-R (n)	CAT (n)	WRAT-M (n)	Writing: Form (n)	Writing: Content (n)	Writing: Total (n)	Grade Average (n)	Teacher Rating (n)
PPVT-R[a]	1.0								
WRAT-R[b]	.75*** (54)	1.0							
CAT[c]	.75*** (54)	.77*** (54)	1.0						
WRAT-M[b]	.62*** (54)	.68*** (54)	.74*** (54)	1.0					
Writing: Form	.48*** (54)	.63*** (54)	.64*** (54)	.54*** (54)	1.0				
Writing: Content	.35** (54)	.47*** (54)	.51*** (54)	.44*** (54)	.63*** (54)	1.0			
Writing: Total	.46*** (54)	.61*** (54)	.64*** (54)	.54*** (54)	.91*** (54)	.90*** (54)	1.0		
Grade Average	.08 (53)	.15 (53)	.27 (53)	.16 (53)	.23~ (53)	.06 (53)	.17 (53)	1.0	
Teacher Rating	.33* (46)	.41** (46)	.62*** (46)	.46*** (46)	.49*** (46)	.40** (46)	.49*** (46)	.54*** (45)	1.0

~$p < .10$; *$p < .05$; **$p < .01$; ***$p < .001$.

[a]Peabody Picture Vocabulary Test–Revised (Dunn & Dunn, 1981).

[b]Wide Range Achievement Test–Revised (Jastak & Wilkinson, 1984).

[c]California Achievement Test (Searle et al., 1992).

Table 5.11. Correlations between 6th and 7th grade measures of scholastic resources

	PPVT-R 6 (n)	WRAT-R 6 (n)	ARI: T 6 (n)	Writing: Form 6 (n)	Writing: Content 6 (n)	Writing: Total 6 (n)	Grade Average 6 (n)	Teacher Rating 6 (n)
PPVT-R 7[a]	.78*** (53)	.72*** (53)	.73*** (53)	.43** (53)	.32* (53)	.41** (53)	.27~ (50)	.34** (51)
WRAT-R 7[b]	.62*** (53)	.91*** (53)	.66*** (53)	.53*** (53)	.46*** (53)	.55*** (53)	.34* (50)	.35** (51)
CAT 7[c]	.70*** (53)	.73*** (53)	.74*** (53)	.61*** (53)	.54*** (53)	.64*** (53)	.46*** (50)	.48*** (51)
WRAT-M 7[b]	.56*** (53)	.60*** (53)	.50*** (53)	.47*** (53)	.43*** (53)	.51*** (53)	.17 (50)	.38** (51)
Writing: Form 7	.53*** (53)	.59*** (53)	.51*** (53)	.57*** (53)	.57*** (53)	.64*** (53)	.37** (50)	.44*** (51)
Writing: Content 7	.29* (53)	.40** (53)	.48*** (53)	.51*** (53)	.55*** (53)	.60*** (53)	.25~ (50)	.31* (51)
Writing: Total 7	.46*** (53)	.55*** (53)	.55*** (53)	.60*** (53)	.62*** (53)	.69*** (53)	.35** (50)	.42** (51)
Grade Average 7	.21 (52)	.05 (52)	.02 (52)	.10 (52)	.24~ (52)	.20 (52)	.54*** (50)	.39** (50)
Teacher Rating 7	.40** (47)	.31* (47)	.32* (47)	.42** (47)	.45** (47)	.49*** (47)	.50*** (44)	.66*** (45)

~$p < .10$; *$p < .05$; **$p < .01$; ***$p < .001$.

[a]Peabody Picture Vocabulary Test–Revised (Dunn & Dunn, 1981).

[b]Wide Range Achievement Test–Revised (Jastak & Wilkinson, 1984).

[c]California Achievement Test (Searle et al., 1992).

Table 5.12. Correlations among measures of scholastic resources in 6th and 7th grades

	6th-grade Literacy Composite	7th-grade Literacy Composite	6th-grade Grade Average	7th-grade Grade Average	6th-grade Teacher Rating of Student's Learning Skills	7th-grade Teacher Rating of Student's Learning Skills
6th-grade Literacy Composite	1.0					
7th-grade Literacy Composite	.90*** (53)	1.0				
6th-grade Grade Average	.33** (54)	.42** (50)	1.0			
7th-grade Grade Average	.16 (52)	.20 (53)	.54*** (50)	1.0		
6th-grade Teacher Rating of Student's Learning Skills	.36** (55)	.47*** (51)	.61*** (52)	.39** (50)	1.0	
7th-grade Teacher Rating of Student's Learning Skills	.47*** (46)	.54*** (46)	.50*** (46)	.54*** (46)	.66*** (45)	1.0

*$p < .05$; **$p < .01$; ***$p < .001$.

students who were retained or who received special education or Chapter 1 services (t (55) = –6.07, p < .0001), (t (51.6) = –5.77, p < .0001), respectively.

The association between sixth- and seventh-grade Grade Average also indicates considerable stability, but at the more moderate level of .54. Grades were less consistent than achievement—an indication of the many additional factors that have an impact on grades. The multiple influences on grades are also attested to by the relatively low correlation between the Literacy Composite and Grade Average in sixth grade and the absence of any significant correlation in seventh grade. Teacher Ratings of Student's Learning Skills showed an intermediate pattern—more stable across the 2-year period than grades, but less stable than the Literacy Composite. The lower stability of teacher ratings and grades across the 2 years may reflect the fact that they were being generated by two different sets of teachers. Teacher ratings also related slightly more strongly to grades than to the Literacy Composite; within grade, these were judgments of the same teachers.

The underdetermination of grades by tested achievement levels in middle school is one of the puzzles we hope further analysis of these data will help us resolve. We found that teacher judgments of students are not as strongly related to students' achievement test scores as to their grades. This suggests, unsurprisingly, that teacher judgments intervene between academic potential and grades. But to what extent do motivational resources account for either grades or teacher opinions of students? What other factors can we identify that might help us understand this drift of scholastic performance away from the trajectory defined by competence?

RELATING MOTIVATIONAL AND SCHOLASTIC RESOURCES

Once we developed the composites for motivational resources and the various measures of scholastic resources, we wanted to know what the relations were among these measures. In correlations among the Literacy Composite, Grade Average, Teacher Rating of Student's Learning Skills, and the five motivational resource composites, only two relationships were evident. Self-Regulatory Motivation (i.e., intrinsic motivation to do well, engagement in school, sense of control over academic life, and feeling supported by classmates) and Anxious Motivation (i.e., being driven by worries about teacher and parent reactions to poor performance) were related to Grade Average in seventh grade. A multiple regression model was tested including both of these motivation variables and the Literacy Composite to predict Grade Average in seventh grade (Table 5.13). Controlling for literacy, both Anxious and Self-Regulatory Motivation were significantly and positively related to grades. Although these associations are significant, they are not very strong. Clearly, motivation is not the primary explanatory factor in the scholastic achievement of these middle school students.

These findings suggesting that motivation does not play a very strong role in predicting scholastic outcomes or teacher ratings are surprising. Of course, one persistent problem in assessing relationships with motivational resources is that the

Table 5.13. Regression models using motivation composites and literacy composite to predict grade average for 7th grade

	Model 1 (SE β)	Model 2 (SE β)	Model 3 (SE β)	Model 4 (SE β)	Model 5 β
Literacy Composite	0.31 (.21)	0.35~ (.20)	0.34 (.20)	0.38~ (.20)	.25
Self-Regulation		0.43 (.22)		0.42* (.21)	.26
Anxious			0.59* (.26)	0.58* (.25)	.30
F (df)	2.13 (1, 51)	3.11 (2, 50)	3.77 (2, 50)	4.05 (3, 49)	
p-value	.1509	.0536	.0300	.0120	
R^2	.04	.11	.13	.20	

~$p < .10$; *$p < .05$; ***$p < .0001$.

state of assessment within the field of motivation is less developed than for academic factors. Perhaps the relationships with motivation are artificially depressed by poor measurement. Alternately, perhaps there is not enough variation on motivational resources—these measurements were taken, after all, during a life stage characterized by disaffection and rebellious tendencies. Although low precision of measurement and degree of variation may both have diminished our chances of finding relationships to motivational resources, nonetheless, our findings contrast with those reviewed previously of a strong relation between scholastic and motivational factors. Our group differs from others studied, however, in being exclusively from low-income families. Perhaps the dynamic of school achievement in this population of learners is simply different, or perhaps there are some subgroups of our participants that show the relationship between motivation to achievement that is more commonly reported and other subgroups that do not.

In fact, we anticipated a much stronger relationship between motivational and scholastic resources. Given that we did not find this strong relationship, we investigated the possibility that there were subgroups in this group for which the relationships among these variables might be very different. In order to pursue this hunch, we carried out a cluster analysis (Everitt, Landau, & Leese, 2001).

DIFFERENT SUBGROUPS OF LEARNERS?

In order to pursue further the question of how motivational resources related to scholastic resources for these students, we carried out a cluster analysis on the 54 students who participated in the seventh-grade data collection. The following five variables were included in the analysis: 1) Self-Regulatory Motivation;[2] 2) Anxious Motivation; 3) Literacy Composite; 4) Grade Average; and 5) Teacher Rating of Student's Learning Skills; A few missing scores were imputed so as

---

[2] These two motivation composite scores were selected because they had the highest alphas and eigenvalues of the five composites generated by the PCA.

to maintain the largest possible group size.[3] The initial analysis generated the possibility of either a 4-Cluster or 5-Cluster solution. The 5-Cluster grouping was chosen because it highlighted contrasts between High-Achieving Girls and High-Achieving Boys. ANOVAs were used to test for significant differences between mean cluster scores on these five key variables.

Scores on each of the variables in the analysis for each of the five clusters are shown in Table 5.14. As can be seen, the largest differences among the clusters occurred in Teacher Rating of Student's Learning Skills. As would be expected, high-achieving students got the highest ratings and low achievers got the lowest ratings. Motivational differences are not as strong as differences in the Literacy Composite or in Grade Average. Cluster 1 groups together the High-Achieving Girls, and Cluster 2 includes the High-Achieving Boys. The students in both of these clusters scored equally well on the Literacy Composite and had similar grades, yet the girls differed in two ways: 1) they had higher self-regulatory motivation, and 2) their teachers gave them much higher ratings as learners. Cluster 3 is composed of Self-Regulated Average Achievers and Cluster 4 of Anxious Average Achievers. The teachers' ratings of the students as learners suggest strongly that the teachers preferred the self-regulated to the anxiety-driven students. Cluster 5 is composed of the Low-Achieving and poorly motivated group of learners—a group whose teachers had very poor opinions about them as learners.

The cluster analysis does, indeed, help us understand the otherwise puzzling lack of relationship between motivational resources and scholastic resources in the group as a whole, as those relationships are quite different within the various clusters. In Figure 5.1, the differences between the clusters are presented graphically.

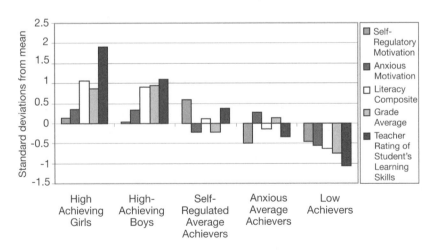

Figure 5.1. Cluster comparisons of five subgroups.

[3]One student was missing Grade Average; the group mean was used (6.16). For students who were missing the Teacher Rating of Student's Learning Skills in seventh grade, the sixth-grade score was substituted. For one student, only the tenth-grade score was available for this variable.

Table 5.14. Summary scores for each of the five clusters (ranges)

	n	Scholastic resources			Motivational resources	
		Literacy Composite	Grade Average	Teacher Rating of Student's Learning Skills	Anxiety	Self-Regulation
Sample	54	0 (-4.34–4.12)	6.16 (0.75–11.00)	39.83 (4.00–99.00)	0 (-3.–2.52)	0 (-3.67–3.20)
High-Achieving Girls	6	1.83 (-0.10–2.83)	8.31 (4.66–11.00)	99.0 (99.00–99.00)	0.47 (-1.14–1.56)	0.22 (-1.64–1.56)
High-Achieving Boys	4	1.57 (0.74–2.50)	8.50 (6.50–10.75)	74.50 (70–76)	0.45 (-0.005–0.97)	0.06 (-1.57–0.92)
Self-Regulated Average Achievers	10	0.21 (-2.04–2.46)	5.63 (2.25–10.00)	52.10 (46–64)	-0.30 (-2.33–1.84)	0.92 (-0.24–2.32)
Anxious Average Achievers	21	-0.25 (-3.89–4.12)	6.50 (3.75–9.00)	30.19 (19–41)	0.37 (-3.06–2.51)	-0.76 (-3.66–3.20)
Low Achievers	13	-1.08 (-4.33–0.85)	4.30 (0.75–8.00)	8.00 (4–12)	-0.74 (-3.27–0.96)	-0.70 (-3.43–2.10)

To develop this graph, all of the variables (Self-Regulatory Motivation, Literacy Composite, Anxious Motivation, Grade Average, and Teacher Rating of Student's Learning Skills) in the cluster analysis were standardized with a group mean of 0 and a group standard deviation of 1. Then the mean for each variable for each cluster was plotted.

Clearly, the complicated relationships are oversimplified in the summary provided in this figure. Indeed, simple correlations between motivational and scholastic resources cannot illuminate the complex transactional relationships among the several components of each. In the next chapter, we present case studies of students who represent each of the five clusters to demonstrate the differing dynamics that operate for each subgroup.

6

Different Motivational Characteristics of Learners

The Carrot or the Stick?

As described in Chapter 5, we conducted a cluster analysis using the following five variables derived from data collected from the Home–School Study of Language and Literacy Development when the students were in seventh grade:

1. Literacy Composite: a composite of student assessment results on measures we administered, including tests of receptive vocabulary, reading comprehension, word recognition, and writing skills.

2. Grade Average: mean of student's reported grades in four core subjects: language arts, math, science, and social studies.

3. Teacher Rating of Student's Learning Skills: teacher ratings of student motivation to achieve, work habits, and level of concentration.

4. Self-Regulatory Motivation: one of the composite scores derived from the motivation scales administered in seventh grade (SPPC [Harter, 1985a], RAPS-E [Connell, 1996], RAPS-C [Connell, 1996], SR [Ryan & Connell, 1989], SS [Harter, 1985b], and PC [Connell, 1985]). A high score indicated strong engagement in school, intrinsic desire to learn, control over academic life, and strong feelings of support from classmates.

5. Anxious Motivation: Another of the composite scores derived from the seventh-grade motivation battery. A high score on the composite indicated that the student was motivated by external factors (e.g., parents and teachers) or feelings of guilt and reacted to academic challenges with worry/nervousness.

Our cluster analysis, using the five seventh grade variables described in Chapter 5, identified the following five groups of students: 1) High-Achieving

Girls, 2) High-Achieving Boys, 3) Self-Regulated Average Achievers, 4) Anxious Average Achievers, and 5) Low Achievers. To better understand how students in these groups were distinguished from each other, we used qualitative data (see Chapter 4 for a description) to develop representative case studies from each cluster. Our intent was to pick an illustrative case from each cluster. For the two clusters of average students, we felt it was too limiting to present only one student each, so we chose two cases from these clusters.

HIGH ACHIEVERS: GENDER DIFFERENCES

Our first two clusters included high-achieving students who had aspirations to attend college. The first cluster consisted of a group of six girls (two White, one African American, one Latina, and two biracial), and the second cluster consisted of a group of four boys (three White and one biracial). As a group, the girls were performing quite well academically, as evidenced both by their high scores on the seventh-grade Literacy Composite and their average grade of a B. Their teachers reported that the girls were excellent learners, displayed good work habits and motivation, and had no problems concentrating or following directions. The group of boys also did very well on our Literacy Composite and obtained even slightly higher grades, with a B/B+ average. However, the boys' seventh-grade English teachers did not rate them as highly as the high-achieving girls on their work habits, motivation, ability to concentrate, or ability to follow directions (99th percentile for the girls versus 75th for the boys). In fact, across our entire group of participants, teachers rated boys as more likely to have learning difficulties ($t = 1.83$, $p < .07$; Porche et al., 2004). In addition, although none of the girls were retained or received special education or Chapter 1 services, one boy struggled to read early in elementary school and subsequently received Chapter 1 services. We found it interesting that despite being rated lower by their teachers, the high-achieving boys' grades were slightly higher than those of the high-achieving girls.

Both the girls and boys demonstrated high levels of Anxious Motivation—anxiety-driven academic coping in response to the perceived authority of others such as parents and teachers. Being motivated by external factors seemed to have translated into positive results for these students from low-income families. The girls, however, possessed higher levels of Self-Regulatory Motivation—strong engagement in general, intrinsic self-regulation and control over academic life, as well as strong feelings of support from classmates—which may have accounted for their higher teacher ratings. Perhaps these teachers had higher regard for students who enjoyed learning simply for its own sake (Lashaway-Bokina, 2000). This gender difference may indicate that girls, at this age, need to feel more invested in what they are studying in order to do well, while boys can still achieve high grades without being as intrinsically motivated (Ablard & Lipschultz, 1998).

Roselyn and Casey

The two students we chose to highlight from these clusters—Roselyn and Casey, both White—attended schools with good reputations and high test scores. The students from the middle school Roselyn attended were expected to continue their education in a high school from which 96% of graduates went on to 4-year colleges; the students from the middle school that Casey attended were expected to continue their education in a high school with an 83% college attendance rate. Both of these students came from intact families. Roselyn lived with her parents in a large city approximately 1 hour west of Boston, while Casey lived with his parents and an older and a younger brother only a few miles from downtown Boston in a metropolitan area. Roselyn's older sister had been awarded a scholarship to attend a nearby Ivy League university. She lived on campus, coming home during school vacations and occasionally on the weekends.

In seventh grade, Roselyn was attending a Catholic school that served preschoolers through eighth graders, whereas Casey attended a public school serving the same grades. Researchers described being impressed with both students' schools. Roselyn's school was described as in surprisingly good physical condition, despite being almost 80 years old. In the waiting area, educational books and parenting pamphlets were available, signaling the school's interest in making visitors feel welcome, as well as in providing resources to parents. Teachers and students seemed to take pride in the effects of recent renovations at Casey's school as well. Students' work was displayed throughout the building, photographs of the students and their teachers lined the hallways, and a reading collage was posted near the main office. Known for its committed teachers, progressive curriculum, and high standards, the school was a lively place the day we visited. It happened to be "character day," which meant that the teachers were dressed up as characters from their favorite books.

Small class sizes were the norm in both schools. Roselyn's English class had only 20 students, while many of the public schools we visited had class sizes of 25–30 students. Students at Roselyn's school came from low- to middle-income families, and the racial makeup of the school was close to 50% minority, with a mix of African American, Asian American, and Latino students. Casey's classroom was slightly larger than Roselyn's, with 24 students. His school was similarly diverse; his English teacher reported that the socioeconomic status of the students "runs the gamut from students who are on welfare to the affluent ones." Casey's school's demographic population was 25%–50% minority, depending on grade level.

On our Literacy Composite, Roselyn did extremely well, scoring above the mean for her cluster. Her high ability level translated into excellent performance in school as reflected by her straight A grades. She was a teacher's dream student. Her English teacher mentioned that she never missed an assignment and was conscientious, well prepared for class, and rarely absent. In addition, he gave her the highest rating possible, 99th percentile, on her learning skills, reflecting his opinion that she was a focused, motivated, hardworking student.

Like Roselyn, Casey was described by his English teacher as being "a pleasure to teach" and as having a great attitude about school. According to his English teacher, Casey was a solid B student who worked very hard to maintain his average. He was described as having good work habits as shown by his organizational skills and reliable completion of homework. However, consistent with the trend observed when comparing the high-achieving girls with the high-achieving boys, Casey's teacher only rated him in the 70th percentile on his learning skills. When interviewed, Roselyn confirmed that she liked school, saying it was more fun in seventh grade because they switched classes and had different teachers, all of whom she liked. Roselyn described science and math (in which she received a lot of homework) as particularly interesting classes, and her least favorite classes were Latin and religion. She reported trying hard in all her classes, with the exception of religion, during which she only "sometimes" tried hard. Classes that were especially challenging for her were social studies and Latin.

Casey also reported working hard in each of his classes to achieve his B average. He commented that he was learning "a lot" or "some" in most of his classes, except for social studies, and he was enjoying most of his classes, except for science, which he claimed was "hard." Another difficult class was English, where he received a lot of homework, just as he did in his science class. For the most part, Casey liked his teachers and believed that they liked him as well.

Roselyn got a higher grade than Casey did in language arts and reported greater enjoyment of reading than Casey reported. These differences between Roselyn and Casey reflect the gender differences found across the group. In seventh grade, girls were more likely than boys to report liking to read and tended to have higher grades in English (Porche et al., 2004). Other studies have shown that, even when controlling for reading ability, girls hold much more positive attitudes about recreational reading than do boys (McKenna et al., 1995). According to her English teacher, Roselyn's reading level far exceeded her grade level. Her teacher felt that she was reading at a 10th- or 11th-grade level. Roselyn was reading her father's copy of *Angela's Ashes* on her own outside of school, for example.

Casey, on the other hand, did not enjoy reading or writing very much. Although results of the school's standardized tests and his classroom performance indicated his reading skills were on grade level, with comprehension and critical thinking skills listed as strengths, his teacher reported his "reading speed" was a weakness. In writing, he was said to be imaginative and to have great ideas, but writing mechanics and editing were areas needing improvement. Casey's English teacher gave him a score of 3 on a 4-point scale when rating his enjoyment of reading and writing. Of interest, Casey rated himself lower than the teachers rated him in both areas. About reading, he explained, "I just don't like to read . . . it's not fun." He elaborated about writing, saying, "We do it a lot in school . . . only sometimes you can get good ideas . . . some stuff isn't that good because you do so much . . . you're stuck . . . sometimes nothing is good . . . sometimes I don't write that good." His teacher seemed to assume that because Casey did his work consistently, he enjoyed doing it; but Casey was frank about his own struggles in school and his frequent lack of enjoyment with it.

By all accounts—from her teachers, her parents, and even her own reports— Roselyn was a motivated student. She scored above the average in her cluster on both of our motivation composites, demonstrating that she was externally as well as internally motivated. Casey, however, was much more internally than externally motivated, meaning he derived pleasure from doing his schoolwork and was not as influenced by his parents' or teachers' expectations and/or reactions. Although there may appear to be a discrepancy between Casey's confessed lack of enjoyment in reading and writing and his answers on our motivation questionnaires that indicated that he was intrinsically motivated, we understand this to mean that Casey realized the overall importance of doing his schoolwork to the best of his ability if he wanted to achieve his longer term goals.

Both students' future educational aspirations were consistent with their teachers' predictions. Roselyn's English teacher predicted that she would attend a 4-year college, at the least, and "likely do graduate work." He based his expectation of high academic achievement on the strong support Roselyn received from her family concerning her school progress, as well as her dedication, her capacity to keep track of her priorities, and her ability not to overextend herself. "She doesn't appear to get upset or worried over anything," stated her teacher, although Roselyn admitted otherwise. When big projects were due, she confessed to getting stressed out and said her parents even thought she worked too hard at times. Her anxiety about doing well and obtaining top grades certainly pushed her to perform her very best in every class.

Similarly, Casey's English teacher said that his family provided strong support for his school achievement. When we asked him if his parents wanted him to work harder or if they thought he worked hard enough, Casey replied, "Hard enough." His English teacher explained that Casey's mother had contacted her several times over the course of the school year just to check in with her about Casey's progress. His teacher felt that if Casey had any difficulties, his mother would definitely be there for him. She took this support, as well as her sense that he was ambitious and goal driven, as a basis to predict that he would attend a 4-year college and possibly even graduate school. She elaborated by saying what a well-rounded student Casey was, and that he had good values, many friends, and a calm, pleasant personality.

Roselyn and Casey echoed their teacher's expectations in the writing samples they produced for us. Roselyn wrote,

Ten years from now I will probably be in college . . . I will be living pretty close to New England, unless I study abroad for a year, then I might be somewhere else in the world . . . I think I'll have become a more accomplished dancer and student. I'll have grown a lot in my mind and body, and I also hope to still be close with my family.

During her interview, Roselyn talked more about her goals, saying that when she got older she would "like to do something with either dancing or photography" and planned to achieve this goal "by going to an art school." When asked if there was anything she could think of that might make this goal difficult, Roselyn replied, "Just if I wanted to get like a job in that, for my career, it wouldn't make much money." In order to get to college, Roselyn said she would need to "do well in high school" and "save money." Roselyn's realistic responses to these questions about her future displayed a level of knowledge and maturity relatively rare in students her age. Perhaps she knew more than most seventh graders about the realities of college because her sister was about to graduate from a highly selective college.

Casey's future educational ambitions were similar to his teacher's expectations as well. When we asked Casey what he would like to do when he got older, he replied, "I might want to do something with numbers, like be an accountant . . . I'm pretty good with that, with numbers." He said he planned to achieve this by trying harder in his math classes, "I'm gonna, like, try and learn a lot." Obstacles to achieving his goals would be "money or something like that, maybe."

Casey was quite consistent in his projections for his future. In his writing sample about where he would be 10 years later, Casey wrote,

I live in Florida now. I'm trying to get a job as an accountant . . . I went to Boston College. When I finished I wasn't able to find any good jobs here in Boston so I moved to Clearwater, Florida . . . I just had an interview with a local agency. They will call me if I got the job. For money I have been working part time in a grocery store.

Compared with many of the other students' writing samples, which contained fantasies about becoming professional athletes or marrying celebrities, his writing sample was both realistic (the need to work part time) and pessimistic (comments about the future job market; Porche & Ross, 2003). Regardless, his thoughts about his future display a maturity, just as Roselyn's did, that is rare among seventh graders.

AVERAGE ACHIEVERS: MOTIVATIONAL DIFFERENCES

The third and fourth clusters included students who were Average Achievers in academic performance. Their motivational resources distinguish the two groups from each other. The third cluster included Self-Regulated Average Achievers and consisted of 10 students, 8 girls (4 White, 2 African American, 1 Caribbean American, and 1 biracial) and 2 boys (1 White and 1 biracial). Students in this cluster were average students (receiving grades of C/C+ on average), and, not surprisingly, the teachers rated their learning skills in the average range as well (52nd percentile). The fourth cluster included Anxious Average Achievers and consisted of 21 students, 9 boys (6 White, 1 African American, 1 Caribbean

American, and 1 biracial) and 12 girls (9 White, 2 African American, and 1 biracial). The traits that characterized this group were low scores in self-regulation, especially when compared with the group's much higher scores for anxious motivation, average ability on the Literacy Composite, and lower teacher ratings than the Self-Regulated Average Achievers received. Surprisingly, however, the Anxious Average Achievers received grades of B−/C+, on average, which were slightly higher than the students in the self-regulated group received.

Perhaps the Anxious Average Achievers' anxiety about schoolwork was what motivated them to achieve better grades. In our population of low-income students, students with higher levels of Anxious Motivation were more likely to achieve high grades than students reporting high levels of Self-Regulatory Motivation, among the High Achievers as well as the Average Achievers. Another possible reason that the Anxious Average Achievers obtained slightly better grades is that many were in special education classes, in which grade inflation might have occurred. In fact, 43% received special education services, whereas none of the Self-Regulated Average Achievers received these services. Approximately 40% of the students in the Anxious Average Achievers group were retained while only 20% of the students in the Self-Regulated Average Achievers group repeated a grade sometime during their elementary school career.

Due to the diversity within both average-performing groups on race and ethnicity, as well as availability of scholastic and motivational resources, we decided to highlight two students from each cluster. Astra, a Caribbean American girl, and Martin, a biracial (African American and white) boy, were both Self-Regulated Average Achievers; and Rochelle, an African American girl, and Stan, a White boy, were Anxious Average Achievers.

Astra and Rochelle

Although Astra and Rochelle were both categorized as Average Achievers, their profiles on both scholastic and motivational resources are mirror images of each other: Astra had good skills on our literacy measures but relatively low grades, whereas Rochelle had poorer literacy skills but better grades. Further, Astra was high on Self-Regulatory Motivation but low on Anxious Motivation, whereas Rochelle was high on Anxious Motivation and low on Self-Regulatory Motivation. Their individual profiles represent exaggerated versions of the average profiles of their respective clusters.

Astra and Rochelle, both of African descent, were living in urban neighborhoods with supportive parents. The schools they attended as seventh graders were challenging. Although the girls differed on each of the five variables used in our cluster analysis, most markedly in their motivational characteristics, they shared the goals of being successful in school and having goals of eventually attending college.

Astra lived with her parents and two younger brothers in an apartment in Boston. Her parents had moved to Boston from the Commonwealth of Dominica before Astra was born. Rochelle also lived in Boston with her single mother and older brother. They lived on the first floor of a two-family house while other members of her extended family lived upstairs.

Both girls attended public schools. In first grade Rochelle began attending school in a suburban system as part of a program promoting racial diversity, while Astra attended school in the city. The school Astra moved to in seventh grade was an exam school (a school requiring an entrance examination in order to be admitted) that served 7th through 12th graders focusing on a rigorous math and science curriculum. The student body was composed primarily of minority students from low-income homes. Many of these students were of Asian descent. Having had an extremely successful year in sixth grade at her middle school, where she had developed close relationships with peers and adults alike, Astra said it was a difficult decision to go to the exam school. Ultimately, after talking at length with her mother about it, however, she had decided to switch to the exam school because it was, in her words, "an honor and challenge to be accepted."

Rochelle attended a middle school serving sixth to eighth graders. Fewer than 25% of her classmates were students of color. Rochelle's mother had been instrumental in getting her into the suburban school program. Acting on her belief that education was of the utmost importance in a child's life, Rochelle's mother had been persistent in researching alternatives to the relatively ineffective neighborhood school that Rochelle would otherwise have attended. Thus, Rochelle was educated in a school system with an excellent reputation, in which 82% of the high school graduates in the district planned to attend a 4-year college. Her middle school had recently been renovated and had an impressive new library. School staff, who worked in collaborative teams, appeared very dedicated. An extensive array of support services was available for students needing assistance in learning or socioemotional areas. Rochelle made good use of some of these services during middle school.

Although Astra appeared to have the ability to do well in school, as demonstrated by her performance on our Literacy Composite, she only maintained a C/C– average in her academic classes. Conversely, Rochelle did not perform well on the Literacy Composite, but she was able to maintain a B– average in her academic classes. Rochelle seemed to be a typical overachiever; despite low-average ability, she pushed herself and as a result earned above-average grades.

When asked how she felt about school, Astra said she liked everything but math. When we probed further, we discovered that Astra was flunking math for the year and this was one of the reasons her grade point average was low. Despite being at an exam school that focused on math and science, Astra was struggling in math and said, "I don't like the way my math teacher teaches." In an effort to bring up her grade, Astra attended extra help sessions after school with her teacher, but these sessions didn't seem to address her problem. Her mother talked with Astra's math teacher, and they agreed that Astra needed a tutor. Her teacher was going to arrange this, but one was not in place at the time of our interview.

Due to her continued difficulties in math, Astra's mother requested that the school evaluate her to determine if she qualified for special education services. The testing revealed no learning disability.

Astra and her mother often talked about whether Astra should return to the exam school the following year. This topic surfaced repeatedly throughout the student interview. In fact, the last question on our interview was, "What advice would you give me if I were trying to decide whether or not to send my child to this school?" Astra replied,

I would try to tell you just keep her in middle school . . . keep her in middle school, let her have an eighth-grade graduation, because you know she could always take the test again [to get into the exam school] . . . then you know she'll be ready and prepared for everything that's going to face her, and she's going to have a lot of difficulties if she starts right away.

Her statements reflected her struggles, the challenging atmosphere she found herself in, and perhaps her regret about deciding to attend this particular school.

Despite her anxiety in her math class, Astra said, "I'm really confident in all my other classes." Overall, Astra was enjoying school, particularly English and science. She commented that she tried hard in all her classes, putting in more than 2 hours a night on homework. She also stated that she was learning a lot in her classes and liked all of her teachers. Astra's English teacher reported that her reading skills were above grade level and, in particular, that she had a strong vocabulary. Despite these strengths, Astra only received a C+ in English the term we visited her. Perhaps this was due to not always completing or turning in her homework.

When asked how she felt about school in seventh grade, Rochelle responded that school was "okay, the work is harder than last year." English and math were her least-favorite classes, but she really enjoyed Spanish and social studies. Her grades in her classes reflected her effort and interest level; she obtained As and Bs in Spanish and social studies while she only received Cs in English and math. As a result of struggling in these classes, she received some extra support in a study skills class. Rochelle also mentioned that she was trying to get used to all of her different teachers and their teaching styles. This proved to be very difficult for Rochelle, as she periodically would be defiant or disrespectful to teachers. In an effort to address these issues, the guidance counselor began working with Rochelle on a regular basis. This support proved to be critical in Rochelle's development.

Astra and Rochelle had very different motivational profiles. Although both were highly motivated, Astra was much more self-motivated, whereas Rochelle was motivated mainly by external factors. Astra's responses during her interview as well as her score on the Self-Regulatory Motivation Composite reflected her independent formulation of high goals for herself. She was a dedicated student who enjoyed studying and learning new concepts and was not overly worried about getting top grades, but rather enjoyed the entire educational process. For

Astra, coming to school with a positive attitude and an eagerness to learn was a daily occurrence. Her Anxious Motivation score was very low, which demonstrated that she was not bothered by average grades and was not motivated by external factors but rather by her own desire to learn.

Conversely, Rochelle's motivation did not come so much from within but from the authority figures around her. Rochelle responded to the expectations of her teachers and her mother rather than an intrinsic desire to do well in school. When answering survey questions about why she tried to do well in school, she responded that she would get in trouble or the teacher would yell at her if she did not do her work or that she felt ashamed of herself if she did not try. Rather than engaging in these activities because she truly enjoyed learning or felt it was important in its own right, Rochelle was predominately motivated by external factors or feelings of shame or guilt. Her need to have others help her stay motivated was further revealed in a writing sample in which she was prompted to write about the biggest success in her life. She wrote about remaining on the honor roll all year during sixth grade.

I was encouraged greatly by my mother and grandmother. Also by my teachers and guidance counselor. My mother and grandmother constantly told me how proud they were of me and rewarded me for that. My teachers would always give me that boost if I needed it, along with my counselor. She also rewarded me by taking me out for ice cream every time I got honor roll. Everyone stayed on me and kept me out of trouble and always provided help for me if I needed it.

Despite their different methods of staying motivated, both Astra's and Rochelle's seventh-grade English teachers expected them to attend college. Astra's English teacher based this expectation on Astra's determination, her positive attitude about learning, and her family's strong support of her school achievement. Her teachers all mentioned her bubbly personality, maturity, inner strength, ability to speak her mind and give opinions during class, and ability to stand up to other students in the face of peer pressure. Astra possessed an insightfulness and confidence rarely seen in students her age.

When asked what she would like to do when she got older, Astra's response was in line with her teacher's expectations. She said, "I want to be a judge . . . and if I can't be a judge, I'm gonna be a doctor." Furthermore, she explained that she planned to achieve her goals by going to school and working "as hard, as hard, as hard as I can." She continued, "I'm going to college, I'm going to finish school, I'm not going to drop out, I'm not going to do anything to hurt myself." She even mentioned specific universities located in Boston that she was thinking of applying to when the time came. The writing sample she completed for us corroborated what she said during the interview. She wrote, "Ten years from now, I would be a hard working student at Boston University or Harvard Medical Center." She demonstrated her maturity, realistic outlook, and knowledge of the educational system by continuing with, "I would work at a nearby bookstore. Trying to start paying off my loan if I had [one] or I could have a full year scholarship."

Rochelle's seventh-grade English teacher rated her learning skills in the average range (41st percentile), which was higher than most of the other students in her cluster. When interviewed, her teacher commented that Rochelle's homework was always on time and complete. Due to this, as well as Rochelle's "on task" attitude and her ability to follow through, her teacher felt there was strong family support of Rochelle's school achievement. She expected Rochelle would attend a 4-year college because she had the desire, support from her family, clear goals, and the willingness to work toward her goals. Rochelle's seventh-grade writing sample and interview responses echoed her teacher's expectations that Rochelle would attend college and become a professional. Her essay about where she would be in 10 years stated, "Ten years from now I'll be a lawyer." In response to the interview question about what she would like to do when she was older, she again responded that she would be a lawyer. The consistency of her response was surprising, as many of the students we interviewed changed their minds about their future plans in the course of an hour. When asked how she planned to achieve her goal of becoming a lawyer she responded, "Sticking with my goals . . . go to college, keep my grades up, and finish high school."

Martin and Stan

Martin, who we considered a Self-Regulated Average Achiever, and Stan, who we considered an Anxious Average Achiever, share some characteristics with Astra and Rochelle, respectively, but Martin and Stan also differ from them in important ways. In particular, although their grades and literacy skills are fairly similar, Martin and Stan differ from Astra and Rochelle in their motivation, parental support, and future goals.

Martin and Stan had a lot in common. Both of them were raised by single mothers living in large cities outside of Boston, and they both grew up in extremely poor homes. At the beginning of our study, Martin's mother had a 12th-grade education, whereas Stan's mother only had a 6th-grade education. Martin and Stan's childhoods were marked with troubles, and their educational placements in seventh grade (which will be discussed later) reflected their ongoing struggles. Martin was sent to live in a foster home with his siblings during elementary school because his mother was deemed unfit to care for them. Stan's mother was abused as a child and lacked parenting skills, so raising her son was challenging for her.

Both boys attended public schools that were large and diverse; their schoolmates came from low- to middle-income families, and 50%–75% of the student body at both schools consisted of minority students. Martin was in a school serving kindergartners to eighth graders, while Stan attended seventh grade in a middle school serving fifth to eighth graders. The schools were located in districts struggling to raise student test scores and increase the number of students going on to college. Sixty percent of the graduating seniors were planning to attend college from Martin's district, whereas only 54% had future college plans in Stan's district.

Martin's seventh-grade reading class was composed of 16 students. Stan's class had only 8 students because it was an "adjustment classroom" for students considered to have emotional and behavioral disorders, all of whom qualified for special education services. Stan received instruction in this classroom for his core academic subjects, but he joined students in the inclusive classrooms at least once a day for subjects such as physical education, art, music, or technical education. Although his teachers said his behavior had improved since his placement in this class, Stan continued to receive detentions and suspensions, adding up to almost 2 weeks of school missed. Martin had also been detained after school on occasion for not completing his homework and for shouting at a classmate. Both boys were seeing counselors outside of school to help them with their emotional and behavioral issues.

Although Stan had difficulty controlling his behavior at times, his English teacher said that he was bright and capable, with reading skills that were on grade level. He always completed and handed in his homework. It seemed to help that he wrote down his daily homework assignments in a homework log, which his mother signed each evening. Stan was rewarded for the work he accomplished in his classroom with a B+ average in his academic courses. Martin, however, earned a C+ average. His teacher rated him as being below grade level in his reading skills, and his homework was only "sometimes" completed. Neither boy did very well on our Literacy Composite—both scored below the mean for their respective clusters—although Stan scored higher than Martin did.

Martin was neither strongly self-regulated nor very anxiously motivated, which may have been part of the reason his grades were average. Although the cluster analysis grouped him with the Self-Regulated Average Achievers, he scored lower on Self-Regulatory Motivation than other cluster members. Stan, who was grouped with the Anxious Average Achievers by the cluster analysis, showed some signs of being intrinsically motivated. His teacher commented, "When he becomes interested in something new, he will become obsessed with it, reading all about it and bringing it in for Show and Tell." Perhaps his ability to focus and his desire to learn translated into better-than-average grades for Stan.

Because their motivational profiles did not seem to match their cluster designations, we explored Martin and Stan's profiles further. It turned out that their teachers' ratings of their learning skills were influential in their classifications. Most of the Self-Regulated Average Achievers had higher teacher ratings than the Anxious Average Achievers. Stan's teacher rating was low, so he was grouped with the cluster of Anxious Average Achievers even though his Anxious Motivation score was low and his Self-Regulation score was high for that cluster. The teacher rating, in a sense, overrode the other variables in the cluster. Martin's teacher rating score was higher, so he was grouped with the Self-Regulated Average Achievers even though his Self-Regulatory Motivation score was one of the lower ones in his group.

Despite having been in foster care, Martin was very well adjusted according to his reading teacher. The only problem, he said, was that "sometimes Martin does not accept responsibility" for his actions. He explained that occasionally Martin would not show up for a detention, saying that he had forgotten about it. However, overall, Martin was functioning well socially. Perhaps this was due, in part, to his interaction with other students his age as well as having some older male role models. Martin played in a squash club after school and had made some good friends there. His teacher told us that local college students were also on the team and functioned as mentors to the younger boys. In addition, during our interview with him, Martin talked positively about his friendship with a Harvard Law School student who had been his Big Brother. Martin and his Big Brother corresponded by writing letters even after his Big Brother moved to Chicago.

In contrast to Martin, Stan was struggling socially. Martin's experiences provided opportunities for growth and development that Stan, unfortunately, missed out on. Stan's teacher commented that Stan did not have many friends in his classroom; instead, he befriended construction workers in his neighborhood when he would watch them working after school. Stan's teacher mentioned that Stan had become friendly with a young man in his 20s who was also hanging around the neighborhood. She reported that Stan's mother allowed Stan to stay overnight at this man's apartment on the weekends when he was having parties. His teacher felt this was totally inappropriate and showed poor judgment on his mother's part, noting that his mother could have encouraged him to play with friends his own age outside of school, which, unfortunately, never occurred. Even though his mother seemed to be able to encourage Stan to complete his homework, his teacher believed that Stan's mother could have done more to assist him in improving his behavior at school, which may have translated into more appropriate friendships and better overall adjustment.

Stan's teacher expected him to complete high school and possibly go on to a community college, saying, "There's no reason why he couldn't." She said that Stan talked about wanting to go to college, and, although she believed him to be bright enough to go on to a 4-year college, she did not know if that was realistic. She felt that Stan would go further in his post–high school education if he attended the vocational high school instead of the comprehensive one. During our interview with him, Stan expressed a real interest in his technical education class. However, unless his behavior improved, Stan would not be admitted to the vocational high school. His teacher said this was the "carrot" she was using to motivate him.

When we talked to Stan about his future and asked him to write about it, he did not initially talk about college. Instead, when asked what he would like to do when he got older, he said he would like to be a car dealer or go into the military so that he could "buy one of those Hummers, one of those big huge jeeps that they got." When he wrote about his life in 10 years, he described himself as having a number of different jobs.

In the past 10 years I have worked at a grocery store then [became] a Ford salesman then a teacher after that I became an electric worker then a plumber then a Dodge salesman then a tow truck worker and a sewer worker.

When prompted during the interview about what he thought he would need to do to get to college, Stan answered, "Get a lot of money." However, he was able to name some local community colleges and state schools that would be cheaper. After acknowledging that college might be something he would do someday, the researcher asked Stan if there were any colleges he had thought about attending, and he said, "Either Harvard or Yale" and that he would like to study "automotive." It is clear that Stan lacked a stable view of his own adulthood, as he envisioned himself working in eight different careers over the span of 10 years, and that he was somewhat uninformed about the realities of both careers and further education.

Martin's teacher, similar to Stan's, expected Martin to graduate from high school and possibly attend a community college/vocational school or 4-year college. He said that Martin "likes being in school, is interested in a lot of things . . . and has an intellectual bent," although he also completed a survey indicating that Martin was mildly underachieving and had some poor work habits. His teacher also reported that Martin's older brother was mechanically inclined and that Martin might be the same way; therefore, it was hard for him to choose between community college/vocational school or a 4-year college when asked about Martin's capability for higher education.

Martin reported during his interview that he would like to "play sports" and be a "car engineer . . . a person who designs or fixes cars." He maintained this line of thinking when he wrote about his future, stating that he would "play major league baseball for the atlanta braves [sic]. . ." and "in the past ten years I have finished high school went to collage [sic] and have gotten a job as a car engineer." When we probed during the interview about colleges, Martin said he might like to attend Michigan State "to play on their football team" or MIT "because I live near there." He was aware that his current grade point average might make it difficult for him to attend these schools; as he said, "I have to get As and Bs."

Comparisons between Stan and Martin and Astra and Rochelle are stark in terms of these students' motivation, parental supports, future goals, and understanding of college, as well as the steps needed in order to get there. The girls scored high on at least one type of motivation, Self-Regulatory or Anxious, while the boys were not particularly motivated either way. Although the boys' teachers reported that their parents were supportive, their parents actually lacked resources and were very limited in their knowledge of how to help their boys succeed— Martin academically, and Stan socially. Astra and Rochelle's parents were more educated than Stan's and Martin's were, making it easier for Astra and Rochelle's parents to advocate for their children when they faced difficulties. The schools the girls attended had higher achieving and better prepared students than did the schools the boys attended, two factors that likely influenced their educational experiences overall.

The girls had much more specific plans about their futures, while the boys were unsure about their goals. Astra and Rochelle's career plans of becoming a judge, doctor, or lawyer definitely required higher education, whereas Stan and Martin's careers as a blue-collar workers and professional athletes did not. Furthermore, Astra and Rochelle spoke at length about their determination to go on to college. They had an impressive and realistic knowledge about the higher educational system, talking about scholarships and loans, and knew that in order to succeed they would have to "stick with their goals" and be "hard working." The boys lacked this type of initiative, focus, and knowledge. They had to be prodded to discuss college, and when they did, it was apparent that they had little knowledge about it. Although all four of these students had grades and test scores that qualified them as Average Achievers, Astra and Rochelle appeared to be on very different trajectories from Stan and Martin.

LOW ACHIEVERS: LIMITED ACADEMIC AND MOTIVATIONAL RESOURCES

Cluster 5 contained 13 students, 7 boys (1 African American and 6 White) and 6 girls (2 African American and 4 White), most of whom were doing poorly in school. Scores in this cluster were the lowest of the five clusters on four out of five variables, with only their Self-Regulatory Motivation being slightly higher than the Anxious Average Achievers. In addition to low scores on the Literacy Composite, grades (C-, on average), and Anxious Motivation, the students in the fifth cluster were rated very low on learning skills by their teachers. By seventh grade, approximately half of this group had been retained or had received special education or Title 1 services.

Todd, a member of this cluster, attended a middle school serving fifth to seventh graders in a suburb approximately 45 minutes southwest of Boston. Most students attending the school were, like Todd, White and from low- to middle-income families. Todd lived with his mother, stepfather, and two older sisters who were attending high school. His biological father lived in a neighboring town, and Todd saw him every weekend.

Typical of students in this cluster, Todd was not having a good year in seventh grade. He hated school, disliked most of his teachers, did not do his homework, and received detentions for not handing in progress reports and his homework. Todd said his mother did not think he worked very hard in school and wanted him to put more effort into his studies. Trying hard in his classes was something Todd said he did "sometimes," although he said he always tried hard in his modern language class. Science and modern language were his favorite classes, and, not surprisingly, his grades were higher in these classes. English and social studies were his least favorite, and, consequently, his grades were lower. During our interview, Todd claimed to be getting passing grades, although his teacher and his report card proved otherwise. Todd said he received three Cs, two Bs, and a D on his previous report card. However, his report card showed he was failing all of his major subjects. This was just one of many instances in which Todd provided unreliable or contradictory information during our interview with him.

Todd's responses during the interview clarified why he disliked school and provided additional information about his struggles there. When asked what advice he would give if a parent was trying to decide whether to send a child to his school, he said, "There's better ones out there . . . keep looking for another place." Then, he continued talking about the need to get along with teachers and students alike:

You know get along with the teachers and stuff but still go along and get along with the kids who are popular, you know how to get along with them . . . you gotta be good at being friends with everybody, not just this group of people . . . it's too hard because the way the kids are . . . they're jerks . . . if you don't make fun of, you'll get made fun of.

When asked if that had ever happened to him, he replied, "It used to." These statements reflect the difficulty Todd had socially fitting into his school and feeling a part of it.

During the school visit, Todd was generally apathetic, not elaborating much during our interview and not putting much effort into the testing either. Part of the reason he scored so poorly on our Literacy Composite was because he did not read the passages on the reading comprehension assessment. It was obvious to the researcher who tested him that he was simply circling the answers without much thought. He seemed to ignore the researcher's request to take his time and do the best he could on the testing. Students were given 50 minutes to complete the 50 questions on this reading comprehension test. Although it took most students at least 30 minutes to complete the test, it only took Todd 18 minutes. Todd's very low score on the reading test in seventh grade showed that he had clearly not put forth his best effort; his reading comprehension scores from fourth and sixth grade were both slightly above average.

Just as we felt Todd could have done better on our testing, his reading and English teachers felt he could have been doing better in their classes. His reading teacher rated Todd's reading skills as below grade level based on his failing comprehension tests during class. His English teacher commented that his writing skills were not improving because he "rarely if at all produces drafts or finished pieces." It seemed difficult for Todd's teachers to determine whether his failing scores were due to a lack of ability, lack of motivation, or a combination of the two.

In an attempt to address the issue, Todd's mother had a psychiatrist test him. She and his teachers were concerned about his difficulty sitting still, his short attention span, his poor organization, his poor concentration, and his disruptive behavior during class, thinking these traits might indicate attention deficit disorder (ADD). Although the doctor's evaluation did detect some signs of ADD, he determined Todd was a borderline case and did not recommend medication.

Todd's reading teacher believed that Todd was receiving strong support from home, citing the mother's effort to get Todd tested as well as efforts he noted during other contacts with his mother. However, his teacher noted how frustrated Todd's mother was because she felt she did not have a lot of control over Todd. Perhaps Todd was receiving mixed messages, his teacher reasoned, and further suspected there had been a period of permissiveness without consequences. Although his teacher believed that it was beneficial that Todd's mother was being firmer, he wondered whether it was too late. In fact, when asked about his future educational expectations for Todd, Todd's teacher replied, "If the course remains unaltered, he will quit when he is 16." He went on to say, "He is not a mean kid. He doesn't act out in frustration but is self-destructive . . . He needs to be aware of the way he is harming himself."

When Todd was asked to write about where he would be 10 years into the future, he wrote,

I will most likely be playing in the NHL living in Dallas or Detriot [sic] . . . Basically for these 10 years I've been playing hockey. I graduated from Michigan St. in 2007 and got drafted!

In line with this, he responded to interview questions about his future, saying he would like to be a hockey or football player. If he couldn't be a professional athlete for some reason, he would "probably be an actor." When asked how he planned to achieve these goals, he said, "Just like follow up with it, you know . . . stick to it . . . can't lose." Todd responded with "Nah" when asked if there was anything that might make achieving his goals difficult or impede his progress. The researcher asked about college when Todd did not bring it up on his own during the interview, linking it to what he had written about in his writing sample. Initially, Todd said he didn't really need college "because there's 18-year-old-hockey players and you don't have to go to school for acting . . . they don't really look at that . . . they look at your talent." When probed further about college, Todd said he would like to go because "what am I going to do afterwards [after his career as a pro athlete or actor]?" He eventually decided he would become an agent or a general manager. Todd did not have detailed plans for achieving his goals, nor was he very interested in attending college. His future plans were more fantasy- than reality-based.

Clearly, Todd was not a very motivated student. The thought that his parents or teachers might get angry if he did not work hard had no influence on his behavior. His responses on our Self-Regulatory Composite showed that he was slightly more inclined to work hard in school when the subject matter was of interest to him; however, his responses show little thought. Just as he had not put any effort into answering the reading comprehension questions, it seems likely he had done the same on this section of the assessment. Todd's answers to our questions about reading and writing further displayed his lack of interest in and motivation toward these activities. Despite initially answering that he liked to read books "some," he later said, "I don't really read them that much." When asked to name a few books he read for fun outside of school, Todd responded, "Well, I haven't read anything recently." He said he got his books from the mail, but added, "I haven't ordered a book in like, five hundred years." When probed, he said, since "third grade." Although he occasionally checked books out of the school library, he described them as "hockey books, and I don't read them, I just look at them."

DISCUSSION AND SUMMARY

These case studies put seven faces on the participants in the Home–School Study and exemplify with descriptive detail some of the findings that we have quanti-fied using data from the entire group. The girls we profiled here were, in general, doing fairly well, whereas the boys, even those of high ability, were more likely to be disaffected and rudderless in relating their current educational experiences to their long-term goals. In the group as a whole, girls did outperform the boys. The girls were generally more positive about school and about reading and were much less likely to be showing behavior problems. These trends echo the research of Duckworth and Seligman (2006), who found that girls earn higher grades due to self-discipline rather than advantage in ability. Group comparisons by race/eth-nicity showed no significant differences on academic performance. Students with strong support from home and who were well regarded by their teachers were more likely to be progressing well in school, even with only average academic skills.

These case studies also show some of the many ways in which factors other than literacy skill can relate to school performance. Among the participants with average literacy skills, those with sufficient motivation, either Self-Regulatory Motivation or Anxious Motivation, were likely to be getting reasonable grades and progressing well enough in school. However, in order to be in one of the high-achieving clusters, these low-income students needed to possess both types of motivation; in other words, they needed to be highly self-regulated but at the same time, they needed to be dependent and worried about the reactions of par-ents and teachers to their performance.

7

Projections of Triumph
and Frustration

One way of summarizing the results of the Home–School Study of Language and Literacy Development is as a set of nested "necessary but not sufficient" relationships. Each of these relationships defines a potential for failure—and demonstrates how much narrower the path to academic success is than the path to academic failure. *Word reading,* the key accomplishment of the first few years of schooling, is necessary to adequate reading comprehension but not sufficient to ensure it. *Vocabulary and oral language skills* are, similarly, necessary but not sufficient to reading comprehension. *Reading comprehension skills* are, in turn, necessary but far from sufficient for continued academic success. Adequate *motivation, planfulness about school, and maintenance of long-term goals* are also necessary but, of course, without adequate reading skills, hardly sufficient. We have, in other words, identified four distinct language and literacy capacities that learners must have if they are to proceed successfully through school. Assume that, for children from low-income families attending schools of only average quality, the chance of failing at each of those is one in four. What, then, is the probability that these children will succeed on all four? Multiplying .75 × .75 × .75 × .75 yields .30— less than one chance in three that a student will master word reading, vocabulary and oral language, and reading comprehension skills while also maintaining motivation, planfulness, and goal-directedness.

Of course, representing the situation as one of success or failure on any of these capabilities is as oversimplified as seizing on 1 in 4 as the chance of failure. Children learn to read words, produce and understand oral language, comprehend texts, and remain focused on the value for them of schooling to greater or lesser degrees. Nonetheless, there is some threshold that children must pass in all of these domains if they are to do well. And the high risk of doing poorly, especially for students with demographic characteristics similar to those who participated in this study, is all too real. According to the latest NAEP, living with limited financial resources and having parents with low education levels is negatively associated with both academic achievement and completing high school (NCES, 2005).

Given the very strong focus on improved literacy outcomes in current educational policies such as NCLB 2001 (PL 107–110), it is sobering to discover that many students with adequate, or even exemplary, literacy skills do not achieve success in school. We found that the transition to middle school was a particularly difficult time for students in our study, and that even our best readers struggled to remain engaged in learning during that time for a variety of reasons. The Matthew effect appeared to operate as hypothesized for the students in our study—but strictly within the domain of literacy. Children who failed to attain an early grasp on language and literacy skills were the students referred out for services and retained, in some cases, multiple times. By high school age, some of these students had little chance of advancing beyond ninth grade. Similarly, students who started out in the top percentiles on standardized tests maintained those high scores throughout their involvement in the Home–School Study. Unfortunately, the associations among standardized tests and grades and completion of secondary education proved more tenuous than we had predicted.

A number of factors determine students' trajectories through school and beyond. Although the importance of academic ability and motivation is obvious, these factors are particularly complex for low-income students who face a range of obstacles in their lives. In this chapter, we explore various patterns of educational achievement for the students who we followed through high school. In assessing final academic trajectories, we examine these questions:

1. What are the educational outcomes for the Home–School Study students in high school?

2. What are the protective and risk factors that may have influenced their longitudinal patterns of success or failure?

3. What can they tell us about how these factors have operated in their lives?

In answering these questions, we are interested in examining a variety of variables that can be considered as hallmarks of academic success, including progressing through school without interruptions, graduating on time, and possessing age-appropriate skills across a variety of domains (e.g., basic knowledge, communication skills, problem-solving skills, flexibility, sense of responsibility, tolerance for others), skills that go well beyond reading comprehension, vocabulary, and writing skills. The goal of the U.S. educational system is, after all, to produce employable and law-abiding adults, informed and thoughtful citizens, and skillful and committed parents. In trying to sketch the participants' development of capacities related to such outcomes, we recognize the need to include the role of socioemotional factors such as motivation and affect toward school (Eccles et al.,

1998; Grolnick, Ryan, & Deci, 1991), as well as the impact parents and other adults may have on students' success (Holmbeck, Paikoff, & Brooks-Gunn, 1995). A key feature of this inquiry is to analyze these aspects of success from the students' perspective.

METHODS

Because of attrition, the final analytic sample included 47 students. However, the distribution of this group is consistent with that of the original full sample for race/ethnicity (67% White, 21% African American, 5% Latino, and 7% biracial), mother's education level at the beginning of the study (54% high school graduates), and welfare status at the beginning of the study (39% on AFDC). The percentage of boys dropped from 50% to 40%.

We collected assessment data in Grades 9 and 10 and a final round of data when students should have been in Grade 12. In the final round, the students who were in school were visited at school. By this time participants were distributed across Grades 9 to 12, reflecting their susceptibility to retention in grade, in some cases more than once. The students who had dropped out were visited at home. Data collection protocols for Grades 9, 10, and 12 included an open-ended interview and a battery of literacy and motivational measures. The Grade 12 interview protocol was similar to earlier versions but with additional questions about transitions after high school. Literacy measures included the Peabody Picture Vocabulary Test–Revised (PPVT-R; Dunn & Dunn, 1981), California Achievement Test (CAT; Searle, Casella, & McCulloch, 1992), and the Wide Range Achievement Test–Revised (WRAT-R; Jastak & Wilkinson, 1984) (described in Chapter 3). Motivational indicators included the Self-Perception Profile for Adolescents (Harter, 1988) and the Rochester Assessment Package for Schools: Engagement Scale (RAPS-E; Connell, 1996) (described in Chapter 5). Follow-up interviews were also conducted with selected students within two years of the final assessments.

A mixed-method approach (Creswell, 2002) was used to analyze longitudinal data collected since preschool but with a focus on later waves of data as students began to make their transition from high school to adulthood. Students were sorted into three academic outcome categories: 1) high school graduates going on to 2- or 4-year college ($n = 16$); 2) high school graduates without immediate plans for higher education ($n = 19$); and 3) high school dropouts ($n = 12$, including some who received a GED). These categories were based on data gathered when study participants were on schedule to graduate after their senior year of high school, as well as on follow-up data gathered 2 years later for students for whom we had current contact information and who had been retained in multiple years in secondary school. We used descriptive and correlational statistics to answer the first two research questions, creating profiles of success and discerning risk and protective factors related to success. Having determined significant risk and protective factors through our quantitative analysis, we then incorporated the students' own descriptions of those factors to better understand academic processes from their perspectives. Content analysis was used to examine interview data (transcribed and coded for content) and writing samples from the students to gain their perspective on their goals and decision-making processes regarding their educational futures and employment choices.

In addition, the students were grouped into five cluster categories that were believed to describe their achievement characteristics: 1) High-Achieving Girls, 2) High-Achieving Boys, 3) Anxious Average Achievers, 4) Self-Regulated Average Achievers, and 5) Low Achievers.

RESULTS

Previous chapters have discussed how student literacy skills are highly correlated across school years, even while those same skills have limited power in predicting later achievement. What factors do help explain students' outcomes? Surprisingly, students who dropped out of school had more in common with those who went on to college, on average, than those who completed high school. As shown in Table 7.1, students who graduated from high school but did not pursue higher

Table 7.1. Mean scores on demographic characteristics and 10th-grade academic measures by final academic outcome

	Dropout	High school diploma	College
Demographic characteristics			
Years of maternal education	11.92	10.78	12.25
Family income category in year 1	$10,000 to $15,000	$10,000 to $15,000	$15,000 to $20,000
Percent male in group	42%	42%	31%
Home Support for Literacy sum score	28.73	25.89	27.44
MLU age 3	3.13	2.85	3.08
10th-grade academic measures			
CAT[a]	57.43	39.41*	64.13
PPVT-R[b]	54.71	42.72	59.44
WRAT-R[c]	67.43	36.18	59.94
Scholastic Self-Concept[d]	3.14	2.77~	3.16
RAPS-E[e]	2.75	2.87	3.03

~$p < .10$, Scholastic Self-Concept scores lower for high school graduates; *$p < .05$, CAT scores significantly lower for high school graduates.

[a]California Achievement Test (Searle et al., 1992).

[b]Peabody Picture Vocabulary Test–Revised (Dunn & Dunn, 1981).

[c]Wide Range Achievement Test–Revised (Jastak & Wilkinson, 1984).

[d]Self-Perception Profile for Adolescents (Harter, 1988)

[e]Rochester Assessment Package for Schools: Engagement Scale (RAPS-E; Connell, 1996).

education tended to have lower scores on standardized literacy assessments and measures of motivation than either their peers who went on to college or those who dropped out before completing secondary school. This might be somewhat explained by the availability of support services that enable students with special needs to complete high school. In contrast, students with high ability but experiencing difficulty in high school related to socio-emotional problems may have had fewer opportunities for support resulting in a loss of talented students in secondary school.

Did literacy skills predict membership in the dropout, high school completion, or college entry group? A very substantial overlap was found among the distributions of the three groups on an assessment of reading comprehension (Figure 7.1), although the top of the range for college-bound students was higher (97th percentile) than that of the other two groups, and the bottom of the range for students who dropped out (7th percentile) and students who completed high school (1st percentile) was lower than that for students who went on to college. It is particularly striking that students scoring as low as the 30th percentile were attending institutions of higher education and that several students with scores greater than the 50th percentile dropped out of school or ended their education with a high school diploma. Although it is encouraging to see that students with more limited comprehension skills were undeterred from higher education, it is disturbing that so many capable students did not complete high school.

Were there interpretable relationships with other indicators of motivation to succeed academically, including self-reported aspirations, self-reported academic comparisons with peers, and support from parents and other adults? In the 10th-grade interviews, college-bound students were more likely to report plans to

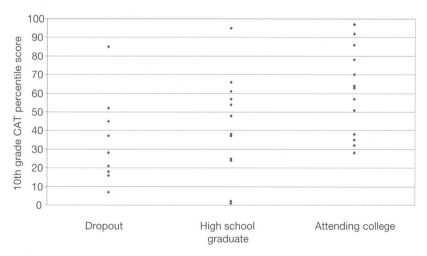

Figure 7.1.   Degree status by California Achievement Test (CAT; Searle, Casella, & McCulloch, 1992) percentile.

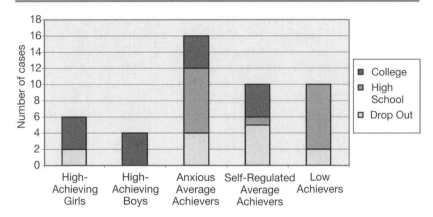

Figure 7.2. Cluster groups by final academic outcomes. (*Note:* One student did not have complete data to be included in the cluster analysis.)

attend college (df(2,38), F = 10.21, $p <$ .0003) and gave more favorable ratings of their grades compared with peers (df(2,38), F = 5.24, $p <$ .0098). When asked "How disappointed would your parent(s)/step-parent(s)/guardian(s) be if you did not graduate from high school?" these students tended to report that their parents would see this as a serious problem (88% responding that their parents would be "very disappointed").

CASE STUDIES

How do these final academic outcomes map onto the clusters we discussed in previous chapters? We did find a fair amount of overlap, in that a larger percentage of the High Achieving clusters of girls and boys went on to college compared with the Average Achiever clusters, and more of the students who dropped out were distributed among the Average Achiever and Low Achiever clusters (Figure 7.2). However, we also saw that two of the High-Achieving Girls dropped out of high school, whereas most of the students in the Low Achiever group completed high school. To take a closer look at the cluster distribution by academic outcomes, we continue our case studies for the students highlighted in Chapters 4 and 6, and also present a case study of one additional student, Emily. (See Table 7.2 for case study students, their cluster designations, and their academic outcomes.)

COLLEGE BOUND: NOT JUST FOR HIGH ACHIEVERS

For the first group, who completed high school and went on to college, we found that early childhood and middle school measures of academic achievement were consistently high compared with others in the group as a whole. They also rated themselves slightly higher on measures of global self-worth and engagement in

Table 7.2. Case studies with cluster designation and academic outcome

	7th-grade cluster	Academic outcome
Casey	High-Achieving Boys	College
Rochelle	Anxious Average Achievers	College Bound
Roselyn	High-Achieving Girls	College Bound
Astra	Self-Regulated Average Achievers	College Bound
Emily	Anxious Average Achievers	High School
Stan	Anxious Average Achievers	High School
Ethan	Anxious Average Achievers	High School
Rashida	High-Achieving Girls	Dropout
James	Self-Regulated Average Achievers	Dropout
Martin	Self-Regulated Average Achievers	Dropout
Todd	Low Achievers	Dropout

school, came from families who were more likely to be working than on welfare, and had parents who graduated from high school. These adolescents talked positively about future plans for college. In addition, many of them were engaging in some sort of productive work activity, such as providing babysitting or doing yard work for neighbors, whereas far fewer of those who dropped out were committed to such activities. The college-bound students also described important adults in their lives, as did the high school graduates, and parent interviews confirmed strong home support for literacy and achievement. Three students in this group had tested into a prestigious public exam school; however, they all transferred back to their neighborhood public schools after a period of struggle in what they described as an unsupportive environment. The college-bound students did not all come from the High-Achieving group, however. As can be seen in Figure 7.2, there were college-bound students from all but the Low-Achiever cluster.

Roselyn, High-Achieving Girl

Roselyn was profiled in Chapter 6 as a member of the High-Achieving Girls cluster. Her original decision concerning high school, made in consultation with her parents, was to continue in the parochial school system that she had attended for elementary school. However, this decision did not provide Roselyn with the academic opportunities that she needed, and she switched to a high school program in the public schools that was particularly tailored for college-bound students and where she could take advanced placement courses as part of her regular program. Her guidance counselor in 12th grade reported that she was "very gifted."

Roselyn applied to a variety of colleges, including several highly selective private colleges, a state college (which offered her a scholarship), and a state-sponsored college of the arts. When asked how she decided what her next steps would be after graduation, Roselyn replied, "I knew I wanted to go to college but I kind of wanted to take the chance and apply to an art school just to see what it would be like." And, in fact, Roselyn decided to attend the arts college. Of interest, in looking back at her seventh-grade interview, we discovered that Roselyn talked about achieving her career goals by attending an art school. She is an example of a student who stuck with and pursued her goals from middle school throughout high school without faltering. When asked what she was most proud of about her senior year, she remarked, "I think I'm most proud of the fact that I've gotten into [the college of arts]. I really worked hard to get my application and my portfolio and everything together." It's not surprising that Roselyn is attending college. With supportive parents, excellent grades, good schools, and an older sister who already maneuvered through the college system, many expected that Roselyn would reach her goal of enrolling.

Casey, High-Achieving Boy

Casey, who was profiled in Chapter 6 as a member of the High-Achieving Boys cluster, was interviewed a year after he had successfully completed his freshman year at a local private urban university. Casey talked about being most proud of earning a 5-year scholarship to the university, which paid for half of his tuition, on the condition that he maintain a 3.0 GPA. He enrolled in the College of Business Administration in hopes of completing a double major in accounting and finance.

In general, Casey liked the freedom that he had socially in college. He did not like the fact that the university was such a big school. This was the main difference between his college experience and his high school experience. His classes were so large that he thought the professors probably didn't know his name, and he felt he was very much on his own. "In terms of work, it's really all up to you. They're not going to push you." In this sense, Casey liked the environment, particularly because there were few "busy work-type assignments." When asked who influenced him to go to college, Casey said that his parents always wanted him to go and that his high school stressed academics so much that it was never really a question. He estimated that 90% of students at his high school go to college. (Massachusetts Department of Education statistics obtained for the year he was interviewed in fact show that 80% of graduates at his school planned to attend a 4-year college.)

For most of his freshman year, Casey did not work while attending school and living in the dorms. Once the school year was over, he went home and worked at his uncle's pizza restaurant nights and weekends as he had done during summers in high school. He also started a full-time summer job working at a local bank assembling loan files, which he considered a short-term job because he felt he would have learned all that he could by the end of 3 months. He reported not wanting to waste work opportunities at a job in which he would not acquire new skills; however, he saw this as a stepping-stone to another job in the business field. Casey liked working at the bank because he felt that it was "getting him in the habit of a real job." It was more professional than what most students his age were doing after their first year of college: He had his own desk with a telephone and computer, and he had to dress up.

Sports were always a big part of Casey's life growing up, and as a young adult he continued to make time for playing roller hockey each week. He told us about his steady girlfriend of 2 years who was attending a university some distance away. They were seeing each other several times a month during the school year, despite the long commute and academic workload. He reported that she was also attempting to complete a double major (pre-med and engineering) and that she placed a high value on education. Although Casey made few friends at school in his first year of college, he spent time with friends from high school when he was home. He said that the biggest challenge he faced in pursuing his goals was that he gets distracted. However, he felt that he had a lot more responsibility than most kids his age and that he "knows when to turn it on." Casey felt that college was definitely an adjustment, although not necessarily harder than high school. He seemed to have achieved a good balance in his life, setting aside time for all those things that are important to him: academics, employment, sports, and his personal life.

Astra, Self-Regulated Average Achiever

Astra was profiled in Chapter 6 as a member of the Self-Regulated Average Achievers cluster. After struggling at the exam school for math and science that she attended in seventh grade, Astra and her parents made the decision for her to return to her middle school for eighth grade and then to enroll in an urban comprehensive high school with a very good reputation. Astra's mother reported that the high school was a good choice because "There was a lot of independent learning, which . . . promotes the kind of self-sufficiency necessary for college." A further advantage of this high school was a process called "junior review," which required all of the students to start planning for their futures. By the end of junior year, they had to go before a committee to present their goals for the upcoming year and for their future. Only after making this presentation did students "graduate" into the 12th grade. Advisory teachers worked very closely with students during their junior year in order to help them make decisions about future options.

Mr. R., Astra's guidance counselor her senior year, met with her "too many times to count." He reported that Astra constantly popped her head into his office to provide him with updates about her college search, to bounce ideas off of him, or to vent about an issue or a problem. Astra did apply to a couple of schools, but she always knew she wanted to go to a local private university with the program in forensic psychology that she was most interested in. This university also had a special program in place to support inner-city students of color, strengthening their academic skills and motivation, and helping them feel comfortable on a college campus. Astra was accepted to this university with a scholarship.

On the writing task in 12th grade, Astra wrote the following about her life in 5 years:

In 5 years from now I plan to be a senior at [name of a specific] university. Since the school has a mandatory co-op program, I will be working [at] the Central Intelligence Agency in Washington D.C. I would like to be a forensic psychologist watching the crime scene, seeing how the person died, and what motive the murderer had. I plan to be living in Boston on campus. Probably [name of a specific dormitory], a major dormitory for all upper classmen at [the university].

The last five years have been difficult. My parents have been somewhat supportive of my career outlook, but sometimes can be fearful of my occupation. Frankly, my father has always disagreed with my decision to work in this business. Other than my parents' over protective nature my life is wonderful.

Not surprisingly, Astra has succeeded in being accepted to college, which was one of her goals in seventh grade. Just as her middle school teachers and her parents expected her to attend college, Astra spoke often of her dream of finishing high school and going on to college. Her determination, maturity, and work ethic seem to have served her well.

Rochelle, Anxious Average Achiever

Rochelle, who was also profiled in Chapter 6, was a member of the Anxious Average Achievers cluster. Rochelle had a very supportive mother who said that her role, with regard to Rochelle's schooling, was to see that Rochelle "gets the best education possible." Although Rochelle reported having disagreements with her mother, she also knew her mother cared about her "a lot" because her mother was always making sure that she did the things she needed to do to succeed. However, school did not come as easily to Rochelle. As an African American girl growing up in the inner city, she faced a number of challenges. Her test scores and grades were average or below, and she needed help with organization and study skills. Nevertheless, due to strong parental support, counseling and anger-management courses, and attendance at excellent suburban schools, she ended up going, in her words, "to a top-ten Black college."

Rochelle's mother established high expectations for her daughter, and these were reflected in all of the schools she chose for Rochelle over the years. Compared with other children in the study, Rochelle attended a highly structured preschool with a strong focus on academic drills and less emphasis on socioemotional development. Initial home visits were conducted in the living room of a modest two-family home where Rochelle's homework station held a prominent place surrounded by alphabetic print posters. Rochelle's mother signed her up for a busing program that took Rochelle from the inner city to a privileged suburb for elementary and secondary school. Being bused to a school in the suburbs was a hardship for Rochelle both in the travel time required and in being isolated among affluent White classmates. Her middle school years were especially difficult; with the short-lived emergence of acting out behaviors on Rochelle's part that threatened to disrupt her academic progress. Rochelle's mother felt that she was the "strongest influence on Rochelle's decision to go to college." And Rochelle consistently confirmed that this was the case in her high school interviews.

In ninth grade, Rochelle was already clear that she wanted to be a lawyer "because I like to argue." She knew that it would be difficult, and when asked in ninth grade what might make it difficult, she replied, "Me slacking off." In her 10th-grade interview, she returned to this theme and mentioned that the thing that would keep her from achieving her goal would be "giving up . . . because after a while sometimes I just get tired of trying." When asked what prevented her from giving up, she replied, "Because my mother'd be on my case about it . . . Plus, if I do, I hate it usually afterwards." By 12th grade, however, Rochelle knew that she would be going to college and seemed eager to make the transition from her suburban high school to a college with many academically oriented Black classmates. Of note, when asked if her mother was pleased with her decision to go to college, Rochelle explained that when she told her mother that she wanted to go away to college, her mother's response was, "No, you need to stay here. You can go to one of the community colleges, but that's it." In spite of her mother's attitude, however, Rochelle felt that her mother "was supporting me the whole time, but she still . . . would prefer that I was closer."

High School Graduates: Alternative Pathways?

For the second group, whose terminal degree was high school, we found average scores on academic achievement measures over the years. An important aspect of these students' trajectories was in their choice of school. A number of them found success in vocational schools and entered the careers they had trained for. Others, however, had only unrealistic or undefined plans for what to do after high school.

Ethan, Anxious Average Achiever

Ethan was profiled in Chapter 4 as one of the students who consistently scored well on our measures but who began a downward academic achievement spiral in middle school that continued into high school. Ethan was a member of the Anxious Average Achievers cluster based on the data collected during his seventh-grade school visit. It was clear from his interviews throughout high school that motivation was a major problem. Ethan and his teachers were unanimous in agreeing that he did not work at school and rarely, if ever, completed his homework. His guidance counselor, Dr. S., mentioned during the 10th-grade visit to the suburban school that Ethan attended that he was "not doing any kind of work at all." Consequently, although both Dr. S. and his teachers believed he was capable of being in the highest level classes, he was demoted to lower level classes. Not surprisingly, Ethan agreed that he was bored in school, although he was enthusiastic about his drama class.

Ethan's attitude about school was clearly colored by his social difficulties. By 10th grade he was letting others know that he considered himself bisexual. His personal appearance was striking. The following was reported by the teacher after interviewing Ethan in 10th grade: "He had dreadlocks, his hair was long, with beads in his hair. He was wearing . . . chains around his neck, some of the necklaces were beaded, more Rastafarian looking necklaces, and the others were real chains that hung down to his waist. He had a goatee." When asked about the groups at his school, he mentioned that he was one of the "freaks" who were in the Gay–Straight Alliance and listened to a lot of music. He said he got along with everyone but the "jocks" and the "Abercrombies," the preppy students, who he described as "mean." In his writing sample in 10th grade he wrote:

The biggest problem is being accepted for who we are. We may dress differently or have opinions contradictory to many people's feelings, but that doesn't make us inhuman . . . I may be an open bisexual but I deserve and demand fair treatment. I expect to be able to attend public school without hearing the words faggot *or* homo *just as it is expected to not hear* nigger *or* chink *. . . I wrote an open letter to the faculty asking how they could accept* fag *and denounce* nigger. *I received no reply."*

His mother reported that by the end of 10th grade, she and Ethan were seeking other educational alternatives for him. Private school was not within their means, so the decision came down to a charter school for students with an international theme in a town nearby. Unfortunately, he was not able to start at this school until January, and the program was not one that captured his interest. During the second year at the charter school, the vice principal drove Ethan to an adult learning center that his mother described as the "Last Chance Café" for Ethan's high school education. Although this effort was made without consulting Ethan or his parents, Ethan's mother reported that the school proved to be a good place for him because the staff were used to dealing with "kids who had fallen through all the other cracks, and they were really determined to not let them fall through theirs . . . That really meant a lot." Ethan was able to obtain a special high school diploma from this school and, his mother reported, intended to begin taking classes at a local community college on a part-time basis. When asked about these plans, however, Ethan mentioned that he had been dragging his feet about applying because he "want[ed] to get out of school." He continued, "I don't want to go to college, but I do, because if you don't go to college . . . you're selling yourself short."

Stan, Anxious Average Achiever

Stan, who was profiled in Chapter 6, was also a member of the Anxious Average Achievers cluster. In 12th grade we visited Stan at an alternative school specializing in working with students with special needs. Stan was transferred to this school at the end of ninth grade for a 45-day diagnostic period after a series of violent acting-out behaviors. After this diagnostic period, he was sent to a juvenile detention center for a year and a half for his violent behaviors and then allowed to come back to the alternative high school to complete his secondary education.

Stan's English teacher rated his reading performance to be well above grade level and noted that "He shows excellent comprehension and has read many books independently." She also stated that his writing skills were on grade level. She noted that Stan had problems expressing feelings and showing motivation to achieve; he had mild problems associated with being withdrawn, disturbing others while they were working, and being overly aggressive with peers. Stan's math teacher also echoed this analysis. Despite these assessments, his teachers and guidance counselor also expressed satisfaction with Stan's behavior in general and his ability to complete assignments, and reported confidence that he would graduate from high school.

Stan's guidance counselor had discussed different options with Stan for postgraduation and was encouraging him to enroll in emergency medical technician coursework. She felt that he had a "50/50 chance" of accomplishing this goal but believed it depended on his emotional stability and confidence.

Stan's English teacher believed he could graduate from a 4-year college because "he has set goals." His math teacher also supported the idea that he could continue education beyond high school because she felt he was a "determined student who will achieve his goal." She noted that "he has a vision for himself."

Stan indicated that he "hated" most of his senior year courses, including math, history, and art, but he felt that English, science, and consumer math were "okay." He named his English teacher as his favorite teacher because he felt she respected him, even after he came back from "lock-up." He felt that some of the other teachers did not treat him the same as they did before he was placed in juvenile detention. When asked what he was most proud of that year, he said he was proud of the fact that he had gotten out of juvenile detention and was still doing well. He said that everyone else he knew that had been released had something bad happen to them (i.e., "got shot" or "kicked out of school"). He was happy and proud to have avoided these outcomes.

When asked to reflect on his high school years and to indicate anything that he wished he had done differently, Stan said he wished he had not gotten into trouble with the law. He also would have rather attended his local public high school. However, he was not allowed to return there after his ninth-grade expulsion. He indicated that he might have taken more challenging courses at the public high school.

Throughout his participation in the study, Stan, an only child, lived with his mother in relatively isolated circumstances, with few friends or family members in their lives. His mother had a sixth-grade education and was unemployed for the duration of the study, receiving support for herself and Stan from Social Security. She also reported ongoing health problems, and her more recent medical needs required Stan to miss 30 days of school to take care of her or take her to doctor's appointments. Despite conflicts with his mother over the years, Stan named her as an important person in his life because she "is there" for him, helping him get out of trouble when he needed it and providing support.

Besides his plans of becoming an emergency medical technician, Stan also expressed interest in going into "criminal justice" work, which he says he "always" wanted to do. Although he had been trying unsuccessfully to get a paying job, he had been able to get a position as a volunteer usher/security guard for a local theater. He reported liking the job because it involved working in security, which he saw as a stepping-stone for work in the field of criminal justice. In the writing task, Stan noted how he had been involved in the criminal justice system for juveniles, but that he had "straightened out" and he felt he was ready to "accomplish his goals."

Emily, Anxious Average Achiever

Emily, who has not been previously profiled, was a member of the Anxious Average Achievers cluster, but unlike most of the students in the study who attended comprehensive public high schools, Emily attended a vocational high school. Despite some challenges early in her high school career, she successfully completed her course of study and graduated from the vocational high school, finding work immediately as a dental assistant. She was especially proud of this because her mother and two of her three brothers had left high school before graduating. Emily said she had consulted with her guidance counselor, mother, and mother's boyfriend about which high school to attend. She felt that she had made the right decision to go to the vocational high school because it "was a better school because my mom went to the [comprehensive] high school and winded up dropping out . . . like everybody who went [there] ends up dropping out."

The year after Emily graduated, we were able to interview her and her mother. Emily's mother was also very happy with Emily's decision to attend the vocational high school. Although, ultimately, Emily's is a success story, she had engaged in many risky behaviors before graduating from high school. Her mother felt that she could have done the work at a comprehensive high school. She described her daughter as "really very bright . . . [but she] needs really strict limits," which were in place at the vocational school. According to her mother, Emily only did what was absolutely necessary to get by in school. She had to attend summer school every summer. However, it was clear she was capable of the work and failed during the school year as a result of lack of effort rather than ability. She displayed her high level of ability by getting As in the summer school courses, and during her senior year she obtained As and Bs in all of her courses. Her mother said that Emily was motivated by the realization that she needed to pass this time in order to graduate.

Emily's outgoing nature made her quite popular. She was a social butterfly for whom school often took a back seat. Experimenting with drugs almost got her thrown out of school, due to the school's zero tolerance policy. After going to the emergency room for a drug-related incident, being arrested, and spending the night in jail, Emily became the "model child." As a condition of staying in school, Emily was forced to enroll in drug counseling. Once again, her family's support along with the strict policies enforced by the school aided Emily in pulling through this crisis.

Emily's mother felt that her daughter might very well have fallen through the cracks at the large comprehensive high school had she gone there. Instead, her teachers at the vocational school put a lot of effort into helping her succeed, and she really blossomed, becoming confident in herself and her career choice. Her mother said that "working while going to school had a positive influence on Emily's academic experience because it gave her more self-confidence and showed her how she would use her education . . . and the practical exposure helped Emily determine that she would like to pursue dental assistantry [sic] in the future." As she became more focused on her future career as a dental assistant, Emily enrolled in a weekend course in radiology and received the certificate long before many of her classmates.

One of the reasons Emily succeeded in graduating was because she had the strong support of her mother and other family members as well as her teachers and guidance counselor. School officials encouraged Emily to attend a 4-year college to become a dental hygienist. Her mother hoped that someday she would do this, saying that she would be "very disappointed" if Emily did not graduate from college. But, at the time of our interview, Emily was content working full time as a dental assistant. She says that she is "most proud of having graduated from high school and of making $20/hour as a dental assistant." She added that her "shop class prepared me well for my current job."

DROPOUTS: HIGH, AVERAGE, AND LOW ACHIEVERS

In the third group, those who dropped out of school, we found some students with low academic achievement who had experienced special educational placement and/or retention throughout elementary and middle school. Others in this group whose academic abilities were average to high had been diagnosed with behavioral/emotional problems and received counseling. Although some were resigned to dropping out of school as early as seventh grade and tended to have only vague ideas about goals for future career paths, others dropped out because they faced obstacles that prevented them from achieving their own goals of extending their education.

James, Self-Regulated Average Achiever

James, who was profiled in Chapter 4, had the academic ability to complete high school and perhaps go on to college, but he dropped out of high school during his sophomore year. His elementary school teachers had consistently predicted that James would go to a 4-year college; his seventh-grade teacher had even predicted that he would go to graduate school. On average, James performed near the 90th percentile on standardized literacy measures across the years. His elementary school teachers rated his reading ability as above average. By seventh grade, however, his failing grades placed him in the Self-Regulated Average Achievers cluster. Even so, in his ninth-grade interview, James said he planned to "go to school to be a psychiatrist" and talked of attending MIT or Harvard because "they are prestigious schools." However, obstacles such as domestic violence, his parents' divorce, and the transition to a new school system, coupled with suspensions from school due to harassment incidents and possession of alcohol, proved to be too much for James to cope with.

Soon after dropping out of high school, James became a teenage father. When he was asked in his ninth-grade interview what might keep him from going on to higher education, he replied, "Well, a complete lack of motivation. There's no reason for me to fail. I had stopped caring."

Rashida, High Achiever

Rashida, profiled in Chapter 4, is one of the two girls in the High Achieving Girls cluster who we believe dropped out of high school. Her guidance counselor told us that she had withdrawn from the large urban high school she was attending at the beginning of her junior year, and we were unable to confirm any further schooling for her. It was, perhaps, not surprising that Rashida had withdrawn from this high school, as the time she had spent there had not been a positive experience for her.

Although Rashida and her mother were given choices at the end of eighth grade about which high school she would like to attend, Rashida did not, in fact, get assigned to any of the schools she had chosen. Instead, as described in the field notes by one of our researchers, she was assigned to a very large high school where "She didn't feel like anyone was pushing her and she felt she had to do everything on her own, and had a difficult time staying motivated."

At the beginning of her second year at the school, Rashida found out that she was considered a 9th grader again because she had not passed enough classes to have 10th-grade standing. Rashida's guidance counselor mentioned to the researcher that Rashida would probably have to take summer school classes. But Rashida said that she had not gotten any letter about summer school and that no one had told her she needed to take it or how to go about signing up. Rashida was reluctant to speak with her guidance counselor. She said she knew she just had to work really hard. The researcher reported: "I really felt like no one at the school was intervening for Rashida. She seemed like she was just trying to figure out everything herself and that the ball was in her court for everything."

Rashida mentioned in her interview during this school visit that she was taking dance classes—hip-hop, African, ballet, and tap dance—4 or 5 days a week for between 3 and 4 hours a session. She said her long-term goal was to go to dance school and be a dancer later in life.

When asked about what she thought she would be doing after high school, Rashida mentioned that she would like to go to college. She said she wanted to do this because she thought it would be "better" and she wanted "to learn more." She acknowledged that to achieve her goal of attending college, she needed to do better in school. She also said that her family encouraged her to think about going to college, although she did not have any particular college in mind. She did say she would like to move to New York.

When asked to write about the challenges she and her peers faced, Rashida produced an intense, well-written essay. She wrote about violence and how difficult it is to live in an urban area. But she also mentioned the school pressures she was facing. She wrote:

Kids my age face a lot of problems these days. Especially if you live in an urban area. Violence isn't unusual where I come from . . . Just this month, I was hit hard with that reality. On May 5 . . . a friend of mine was at a party. I don't know what events led up to it but at 11:50 P.M. he was pronounced dead from multiple bullet wounds. I'll never forget the date or time because that was when the truth of what was going on in my neighborhood really hit me. Not only are things like this a problem but on top of that we are weighed down with school, MCAS [Massachusetts Comprehensive Assessment System], expectations, tests and problems at home. With all those problems [adding] up together, us kids have it really hard these days.

Martin, Self-Regulated Average Achiever

Martin, who was profiled in Chapter 6, had a smooth transition to the local public high school. However, he didn't get the house (school-within-a-school) designation that he wanted because he had signed up past the deadline. His mother explained that this happened because she had been contemplating enrolling him in a parochial high school until she found out that she could not afford it.

Martin's guidance counselor felt that Martin could "definitely" graduate from high school and would "eventually" graduate from college. However, Martin was getting Ds and Fs in some of his classes, and, therefore, he felt that Martin might have to go to a community college. His English teacher, however, felt that Martin would not go beyond high school because of his "lack of motivation and interest in school."

When asked about future plans, Martin mentioned playing professional baseball or becoming a carpenter, but he also thought it was "very likely" that he would go to college so that he wouldn't "throw his life away." Martin mentioned the names of two highly selective colleges, one of which had been "recruiting" at his high school. The interviewer remarked: "It is . . . interesting that while he is determined to go to college, his two career goals (baseball and carpentry) do not require it. Martin does not seem to notice this discrepancy." When asked what might keep him from reaching his goals, Martin mentioned "doing drugs or failing out of school."

When we tried to contact Martin for a final high school interview 2 years later, we found that he was no longer living at home and had again been moved into the foster care system. His guidance counselor informed us that he had dropped out of school.

Todd, Low Achiever

Todd, who was profiled in Chapter 6, was designated as a member of the Low Achievers cluster in seventh grade based on his grades, his standardized test scores, and his motivation scores. After starting high school at his local public school, Todd was moved to an alternative program due to continued concerns about his possible ADD and his failure to make an effort in school. The alternative program was very small, and Todd reported that he had a hard time feeling that he could grow there because it was such a small program with so few options for the students. When he returned to the school the next year, he stayed for only a week before dropping out. He reported that he had decided to drop out because a guidance counselor had told him that if he graduated from that school he could only go to a community college, not a 4-year college. Consequently, he did not believe that it was worth his time to continue. Unfortunately, this behavior matched the expectations of both his seventh-grade reading teacher ("If the course remains unaltered, he will quit when he is 16") and his mother ("I always knew Todd would quit school when he was 16").

In an interview conducted when Todd was 19, he indicated that he had taken the GED examination but failed because he did not do well on the math section. By this time, he had held down a variety of jobs, including working at the local Boys' and Girls' Club, where he had spent considerable time while growing up; working as a security guard at a mall; and working in a liquor store. However, he did not hold these jobs for very long and didn't consider them as careers. He talked about plumbing or joining the police academy as options but admitted that he had done none of the research necessary to find out how to go about getting started with either. After living independently for a short time, he had moved back into his mother's house because he could not meet his car payments and had not been paying his rent. At the time of the most recent interview, Todd was unemployed. The interviewer reported the following as the only challenge that Todd had noticed in trying to achieve his goals:

The way specific people will look down at you just because you don't have a high school degree . . . Some people think that makes you a complete loser . . . and I know with me and other people that's not always the case.

In answer to a question about long-term goals, Todd mentioned that he wanted to go to school and figure out what he was going to do for the rest of his life.

DIFFERENT TRAJECTORIES, DIFFERENT OUTCOMES

This analysis suggests a number of profiles of academic trajectories for participants in the study: 1) those who sustain their motivation and academic standing through secondary school and into higher education, 2) those who struggle through middle school yet recover academically and go on to higher education, 3) those who struggle through middle school and take the initiative to move to alternative high school settings where they can define their career goals and receive preparation for a service-sector job, and 4) those of varying ability who are unable to complete high school for a variety of reasons. Protective factors that may influence outcomes for the first three profiles include academic and emotional support from parents and other adults and proactive decision making about high school selection. Risk factors for the fourth profile include multiple transitions between schools, family disruption, and socioemotional issues. These student narratives deepen our understanding of the scope of these protective and risk factors as played out in the context of their lives.

8

Lessons Learned and Lessons Needed

Seeking the Missing Puzzle Pieces

The researcher's summary of this study would be fairly unambiguous: Understanding literacy development is challenging, and understanding academic achievement even harder. Literacy is crucial to academic achievement, and many other factors are as well. Although excellent literacy instruction and support during the preschool and primary grades can decrease the likelihood of academic failure, many students also need rich and explicit comprehension instruction in the middle and secondary grades, as well as the sort of attention from adults that ensures high levels of motivation, engagement with school, goal setting, and planning abilities. It is unlikely that adolescents who feel that they have no supportive, caring adults in their lives will persist through the challenges of high school.

The policy maker or practitioner might have more trouble, however, deciding what all this means. In fact, the complexity of the system and the long list of important predictors might derail any policy or practice response by making the situation seem intractable. If there are so many factors at play, where does one start? If so many pieces of the puzzle are missing, should it just be discarded? We hope that invoking an appropriate level of alarm about educational outcomes is an effective step in moving toward solutions, and with some haste. In this chapter, we attempt to deflect the throwing-up-the-hands response by linking our findings directly to some suggestions for practice and policy designed to improve adolescents' chances of academic success.

THE CURRENT PRACTICE AND POLICY CONTEXT

Although middle and secondary school has received increased attention in the first decade of the 21st century as the locus of great educational challenge[1], current policies (especially federal policies) and the currently available research base remain more strongly focused on the early years. Many good programs are available to bolster early literacy achievement for low-income children at risk for delays (e.g., Early Head Start and Head Start at the federal level). Policy attention to reading instruction in the primary grades is at an all-time high as a result of the Reading First provisions of the No Child Left Behind Act of 2001 (PL 107-110). And the research base guiding prevention, intervention, and instructional programs for children up to age 8 is robust (National Reading Panel, 2000; Snow et al., 1998).

Unfortunately, no middle or secondary school equivalent of Head Start exists, and research-based guidance about literacy instruction after the primary grades is neither as convergent nor as rich as for the primary grades. These lacunae may reflect the inoculation theory—the default assumption that success in early literacy acquisition will automatically lead to adequate reading comprehension and the capacity to learn through reading. Both an understanding of the educational challenges of the later grades and the data we have presented in this book call this assumption into question.

The growing anxiety about the academic fate of high-risk adolescents has led to initiatives of three sorts: some focused on raising standards, some focused on the contexts in which adolescents study, and some focused on the kind of instruction they are receiving. The standards-related efforts have had, most would argue, mixed effects. These involve requiring passing performance on high school accountability assessments in order to receive a high school diploma. This has now been adopted by 19 states, with plans to phase in exit examinations by 2012 in 7 more states. Although such efforts are widely endorsed by the business community interested in ensuring that a high school diploma means something, these efforts are likely to generate increased academic effort or involvement only from students whose skills put passing the test within reach and who already understand the value of a high school diploma. For others, indeed for a few students they in our study, the requirement might actually encourage dropping out early if it seems unlikely that they will get the credentials they seek, even with additional years of study. Furthermore, the use of accountability assessments in secondary schools increases the incentives for schools to push out failing or marginal students before graduation (Losen, 2004).

---

[1]See, for example, the efforts of the Alliance for Excellent Education (http://www.all4ed.org), the Carnegie Corporation of New York's education program (http://www.carnegie.org/sub/program/education.html), and the Bill and Melinda Gates Foundation's education program (http://www.gatesfoundation.org/Education).

The context-focused efforts have almost all involved reducing school size to promote student success. Estimates of ideal school size range from 600–900 students (Lee & Smith, 1997) to 200 students or fewer (Noguera, 2002; Vander Ark, 2002). In cases in which large schools (those serving more than 3,000 students) could not be physically altered, reforms have been put in place through academy models to create smaller schools within the larger schools. The New Millennium High School model in Florida appeared to influence increases in some aspects of student achievement, staff morale, and improved student–teacher relationships (Mullen, 2002), for example. Similarly, the Coalition Campaigns School Project in New York City has shown improved academic achievement, attendance, and higher graduation rates as a result of reform that disaggregated a comprehensive high school into five smaller units (Darling-Hammond, Ancess, & Ort, 2002). One mechanism by which smaller schools promote higher learning is through a link with more positive teacher attitudes, which in turn influence higher student achievement (Lee & Loeb, 2000). Certainly the kinds of alienation from adults reported by the dropouts in our study would be less likely to emerge or persist in smaller school communities. Nonetheless, the research findings from these small schools' efforts are scanty and at best suggest modest effects. Most of the school downsizing projects have been undertaken without any attention to evaluation, with the result that little is known about taking these efforts to scale, adapting them to different settings, or the negative effects these efforts might have on the richness of the academic program offered.

Many of the small-school reform models have focused more on the structural than on the pedagogical features of the small schools. The third set of initiatives, focused on improving adolescents' academic outcomes, is based on the hope that engagement in school can be maintained if challenging, relevant, content-area instruction is offered together with support for the development of sophisticated literacy skills so that students can, indeed, have access to the enriched content. These efforts are in response to the robust finding that adolescents' motivation to learn and interest in the materials being read is related to their school performance. Programs that involve adolescents in authentic reading and learning (e.g., the science project approach developed by Bouillion and Gomez [2001] or the Reading for Understanding model of Schoenbach, Greenleaf, Cziko, and Hurwitz [1999]) offer considerable promise in this regard, although again, efforts to extend such programs to large numbers of schools are needed.

Current policies to improve adolescent achievement have not generated notable improvements for significant numbers of students. It may well be, of course, that higher standards, smaller schools, and better teaching all help, but these efforts have effects too small to notice. Or it may be that all would help but only if they acted in combination. Perhaps, if high standards were enforced— but in a context in which personal relationships with adults, guidance about short-term and long-term planning, challenging curriculum, and academic support were available—the achievement of high school students would rise, and their risk of dropping out or of graduating with limited knowledge and skills would decline.

LESSONS FROM THIS STUDY

There is no denying that some results from this study are extremely discouraging. Many of the student participants described unrealistic life plans, whereas others showed a total absence of planning abilities. The case studies provide too many examples of children growing up in homes in which adults did not have the personal or financial means to provide support, and even more examples of students who could find nothing to connect them to their teachers or their classmates in school. Most distressing is the subgroup of high school dropouts with high literacy skills—young people with the capacities to do well in college or advanced technical training—who were derailed from productive pathways by their disaffection from school.

As noted in Chapter 7, the college-bound students were not all high achievers. In fact, students scoring as low as the 30th percentile on our literacy assessments were attending institutions of higher education—suggesting that the American promise of higher education for all is being fulfilled, perhaps by the availability of institutions of higher education serving many different needs. The students considered low-achieving college goers appeared to have important assets; they had not only a high school diploma but also the motivation, planning, and familial support needed to apply and get into college. Nonetheless, it seems likely that these students will join the multitudes required to take remedial academic reading and writing classes at institutions supposedly devoted to higher learning and will, as a result, take longer to graduate, or possibly become discouraged and exit without a degree[2]. Careful attention to the design of academic support programs in relatively nonselective colleges and universities will be necessary to protect the assets such students represent until we start to seriously address reading instruction in the middle and secondary grades.

Some results were also surprising and encouraging. We found positive effects of both special education and vocational education on adolescents' life courses. Although students in special education might be presumed to have greater academic challenges than others, they reported higher motivation, greater interest in school, and more positive attitudes. Perhaps the access to smaller classes or closer relationships with adults provided by the special education programs served these students well. Similarly, the small number of students in our study who attended

---

[2]Many efforts are directed toward solving these issues. For example, the possibility of ameliorating some or all of these conditions by providing financial and other support has been the focus of an effort by the Say Yes to Education Foundation (http://www.sayyestoeducation.org/index.html), which has offered free college tuition to inner-city students who have been able to successfully complete their high school education.

vocational high schools all received their high school diplomas and expressed higher than average satisfaction with their schooling.

Another surprising finding was that students in the group who dropped out of high school had more in common, in some ways, with those who went on to college than with those who ended their education with high school. Some of the participants who dropped out of high school, for example, had literacy scores well above the 50th percentile. Perhaps we should reexamine the pool of high school dropouts as a source of recoverable talent. Of course, some percentage of them do have limited academic skills, but the subset with good literacy skills might, once they emerge from the disaffection of adolescence, have considerable potential for further education and productive employment.

Far too many students in our group had adequate or excellent academic skills but ended up struggling in high school, either dropping out or, like Ethan, getting a diploma only because alternative programs were available. Although this suggests the importance of maintaining these alternative programs, they represent a tiny bandage on a gaping wound. Configuring schools so that students such as Ethan, James, and Martin would feel socially secure, intellectually challenged, and affectively engaged would reduce the incidence of dropouts and the need for alternative programs, and would unleash and channel considerable academic potential.

The students who ended up attending college articulated those plans to us years before the actual applications were due and reported, as well, that their parents would be very disappointed if they did not attend college. Getting to college, in other words, is a process that starts with discussion of the possibility and explicitness about the expectation well before high school. Conversations about college plans can be started when children are in elementary school. But in high school, careful monitoring of student progress and attention to the process of decision making is crucial. This is the kind of resource that some high schools offer and others do not. Consider Astra's experience in her school, where the junior review of students' long-term plans was a prerequisite to 12th-grade entry—she had access to a junior year advisory teacher, and she met with her senior guidance counselor "too many times to count." Contrast that with the experience of Rashida, who was not even properly informed about the courses she needed or her summer school options to achieve sophomore standing. These inequities in access to adults interested in and knowledgeable about helping students navigate through high school and beyond may explain why some students get so far off track that they completely lose their way (Noguera & Wing, 2006).

The stories of the three students in the group we studied who achieved entry into a prestigious public exam school were particularly poignant. All of them ended up back in neighborhood schools, and all reported academic struggles and an absence of support in the exam school. All of these students were academically capable of succeeding in the exam school, but they lacked some of the academic and familial resources their classmates there enjoyed. The exam school environment could have been a pathway to high success rather than an experience of lowered self-esteem for these adolescents had the school taken more responsibility to provide support to them.

In describing the school life trajectories of the students in the Home–School Study, we have emphasized that the path to academic success is much narrower than the path to failure. But some cases demonstrate that the path to success can have some detours. Emily, for example, experimented in high school with drugs and other risky behaviors, did the minimum to get by, and had to attend summer school every year. Ultimately, though, she graduated with the vocational qualification she wanted, immediately secured a job, and was contemplating studying for a higher qualification after a few years of work. Emily clearly benefited from her mother's willingness to set limits, from the structure offered by her vocational school, and from the proximity of her employment goal. Had Emily been sanctioned more severely for her transgressions, for example by expulsion required by zero tolerance policies (Verdugo, 2002), we can only assume that the outcome would not have been as happy.

The case studies we have presented throughout this book confirm results collected by others suggesting that academic and emotional support from parents and other adults, as well as proactive high school selection, constitute protective factors for adolescent learners. Multiple transitions between schools, family disruptions, and socio-emotional disorders constitute risk factors that can derail the progress even of students with strong literacy skills and academic potential. This longitudinal look at groups of successful and less successful students shows the interplay of protective factors with risks in influencing academic achievement. Moreover, taking a phenomenological view of this process by using the students' own narratives helps us understand complexities in student lives that are often neglected by the adults who make the rules.

References

Ablard, K.E., & Lipschultz, R.E. (1998). Self-regulated learning in high-achieving students: Relations to advanced reasoning, achievement goals, and gender. *Journal of Educational Psychology, 90*(1), 94–101.

Alexander, K.L., Entwistle, D.R., & Horsey, C.S. (1997). From the first grade forward: Early foundations of high school dropout. *Sociology of Education, 70*(2), 87–107.

Anderman, E. M. (1998). The middle school experience: Effects on the math and science achievement of adolescents with LD. *Journal of Learning Disabilities, 31*(2), 128–138.

Anderman, E.M. (2002). School effects on psychological outcomes during adolescence. *Journal of Educational Psychology, 94*(4), 795–809.

Anderman, E.M., Maehr, M.L., & Midgley, C. (1999). Declining motivation after the transition to middle school: Schools can make a difference. *Journal of Research & Development in Education, 32*(3), 131–147.

Anderman, L.H., & Midgley, C. (1998). *Motivation and middle school students. ERIC Digest.* Champaign, IL: ERIC Clearinghouse on Elementary and Early Childhood Education.

Anderson, R.C., & Freebody, P. (1981). Vocabulary knowledge. In J.T. Guthrie (Ed.), *Comprehension and teaching: Research reviews* (pp. 77–117). Newark, DE: International Reading Association.

Ascher, C., & Fruchter, N. (2001). Teacher quality and student performance in New York City's low-performing schools. *Journal of Education for Students Placed at Risk (JESPAR), 6*(3), 199–214.

Askew, S., & Ross, C. (1988). *Boys don't cry: Boys and sexism in education.* Philadelphia: Open University Press.

Baker, L., Scher, D., & Mackler, K. (1997). Home and family influences on motivations for reading. *Educational Psychologist, 32*(2), 69–82.

Baker, L., & Wigfield, A. (1999). Dimensions of children's motivation for reading and their relations to reading activity and reading achievement. *Reading Research Quarterly, 34*(4), 452–477.

Battin-Pearson, S., Newcomb, M.D., Abbott, R.D., Hill, K.G., Catalano, R.F., & Hawkins, J.D. (2000). Predictors of early high school dropout: A test of five theories. *Journal of Educational Psychology, 92*(3), 568–582.

Beals, D.E. (2001). Eating and reading: Links between family conversations with preschoolers and later language and literacy. In D.K. Dickinson & P.O. Tabors (Eds.), *Beginning literacy with language: Young children learning at home and school* (pp. 75–92). Baltimore: Paul H. Brookes Publishing Co.

Beck, I., & McKeown, M. (1991). Conditions of vocabulary acquisition. In R. Barr, M. Kamil, P. Mosenthal, & P.D. Pearson (Eds.), *Handbook of reading research* (Vol. 2, pp. 789–814). New York: Longman.

Biancarosa, G., & Snow, C.E. (2006). *Reading next: A vision for action and research in middle and high school literacy: A Report to Carnegie Corporation of New York* (2nd ed.). Washington, DC: Alliance for Excellent Education.

Bouillion, L.M., & Gomez, L.M. (2001). Connecting school and community with science learning: Real world problems and school-community partnerships as contextual scaffolds. *Journal of Research in Science Teaching, 38*(8), 878–898.

Bradford, D.J. (1999). Exemplary urban middle school 'teachers' use of the five standards of effective teaching. *Teaching and Change, 7*(1), 53–78.

Catts, H.W., Fey, M.E., Tomblin, J.B., & Zhang, X. (2002). A longitudinal investigation of reading outcomes in children with language impairments. *Journal of Speech Language & Hearing Research, 45,* 1142–1157.

Catts, H.W., Fey, M.E., Zhang, X., & Tomblin, J.B. (1999). Language basis of reading and reading disabilities: Evidence from a longitudinal investigation. *Scientific Studies of Reading, 3*(4), 331-361.

Chevalier, A., & Lanot, G. (2002). The relative effect of family characteristics and financial situation on educational achievement. *Education Economics, 10*(2), 165–181.

Chung, H., Elias, M., & Schneider, K. (1998). Patterns of individual adjustment changes during middle school transition. *Journal of School Psychology, 36*(1), 83–101.

Coley, R.J. (2001). *Differences in the gender gap: Comparisons across racial/ethnic groups in education and work.* Princeton, NJ: Educational Testing Service.

Conlin, M. (2003, May 26). The new gender gap: From kindergarten to grad school, boys are becoming the second sex. *BusinessWeek,* p. 76.

Connell, J.P. (1985). A new multidimensional measure of children's perception of control. *Child Development, 56,* 1018–1041.

Connell, J.P. (1996). *Rochester Assessment Package for Schools.* Rochester, NY: Institute for Research and Reform in Education.

Connell, R.W. (1995). *Masculinities.* Berkeley, CA: University of California Press.

Cote, L.R. (2001). Language opportunities during mealtimes in preschool classrooms. In D.K. Dickinson & P.O. Tabors (Eds.), *Beginning literacy with language: Young children learning at home and school* (pp. 205–221). Baltimore: Paul H. Brookes Publishing Co.

Creswell, J.W. (2002). *Research design: Qualitative, quantitative, and mixed methods approaches.* Thousand Oaks, CA: Sage Publications.

CTB Macmillan/McGraw-Hill. (1992). *California Achievement Tests* (CAT, 5th ed.). Monterey, CA: Macmillan/McGraw-Hill.

Cunningham, A.E., Perry, K.E., & Stanovich, K.E. (2001). Converging evidence for the concept of orthographic processing. *Reading and Writing: An Interdisciplinary Journal, 14*(5–6), 549–568.

Cunningham, A.E., & Stanovich, K.E. (1997). Early reading acquisition and its relation to reading experience and ability 10 years later. *Developmental Psychology, 33*(6), 934–945.

Darling-Hammond, L., Ancess, J., & Ort, S. W. (2002). Reinventing high school: Outcomes of the Coalition Campus Schools Project. *American Educational Research Journal, 39*(3), 639–673.

Davidson, R., Kline, S., & Snow, C.E. (1986). Definitions and definite noun phrases: Indicators of children's decontextualized language skills. *Journal of Research in Childhood Education, 1,* 37–48.

Davis, F. (1968). Research in comprehension in reading. *Reading Research Quarterly, 3,* 499–545.

Denton, K., & West, J. (2002). *Children's reading and mathematics achievement in kindergarten and first grade.* (NCES 2002125). U.S. Department of Education, National Center for Education Statistics. Washington, DC: U.S. Government Printing Office.

DeTemple, J.M. (2001). Parents and children reading books together. In D.K. Dickinson & P.O. Tabors (Eds.), *Beginning literacy with language: Young children learning at home and school* (pp. 31–51). Baltimore: Paul H. Brookes Publishing Co.

Dickinson, D.K. (2001a). Book reading in preschool classrooms: Is recommended practice common? In D.K. Dickinson & P.O. Tabors (Eds.), *Beginning literacy with language: Young children learning at home and school* (pp. 175–203). Baltimore: Paul H. Brookes Publishing Co.

Dickinson, D.K. (2001b). Large-group and free-play times: Conversational settings supporting language and literacy development. In D.K. Dickinson & P.O. Tabors (Eds.), *Beginning literacy with language: Young children learning at home and school* (pp. 223–255). Baltimore: Paul H. Brookes Publishing Co.

Dickinson, D.K. (2001c). Putting the pieces together: Impact of preschool on children's language and literacy development in kindergarten. In D.K. Dickinson & P.O. Tabors (Eds.), *Beginning literacy with language: Young children learning at home and school* (pp. 257–287). Baltimore: Paul H. Brookes Publishing Co.

Dickinson, D.K., & Snow, C.E. (1987). Interrelationships among prereading and oral language skills in kindergartners from two social classes. *Early Childhood Research Quarterly, 2*(1), 1–25.

Dickinson, D.K., & Tabors, P.O. (Eds.). (2001). *Beginning literacy with language: Young children learning at home and school.* Baltimore: Paul H. Brookes Publishing Co.

Duckworth, A.L., & Seligman, M.E.P. (2006). Self-discipline gives girls the edge: Gender in self-discipline, grades, and achievement test scores. *Journal of Educational Psychology, 98*(1), 198–208.

Duke, N.K., & Kays, J. (1998). "Can I say 'Once upon a time'?": Kindergarten children developing knowledge of information book language. *Early Childhood Research Quarterly, 13*(2), 295–318.

Dunn, L., & Dunn, L. (1981). *Peabody Picture Vocabulary Test–Revised.* Circle Pines, MN: American Guidance Service.

Durkin, D. (1979). What classroom observations reveal about reading comprehension instruction. *Reading Research Quarterly, 14*(4), 481–533.

Early Head Start Research and Evaluation Project. (2002). *Making a difference in the lives of infants and toddlers and their families: The impacts of Early Head Start.* Washington, DC: Department of Health and Human Services.

Eccles, J.S., Adler, T.F., Futterman, R., Goff, S.B., Kaczala, C.M., Meece, J.L., et al. (1983). Expectancies, values, and academic behaviors. In J.T. Spencer (Ed.), *Achievement and achievement motivation* (pp. 75–146). San Francisco: W.J. Freeman.

Eccles, J.S., & Midgley, C. (1989). Stage/environment fit: Developmentally appropriate classrooms for early adolescents. In R.E. Ames & C. Ames (Eds.), *Research on motivation in education* (Vol. 3). New York: Academic Press.

Eccles, J.S., Wigfield, A., Midgley, C., Reuman, D., Iver, D.M., & Feldlaufer, H. (1993). Negative effects of traditional middle schools on students' motivation. *Elementary School Journal, 93*(5), 553–574.

Eccles, J.S., Wigfield, A., & Schiefele, U. (1998). Motivation to succeed. In N. Eisenberg (Ed.), *Handbook of child psychology: Vol. 3. Social, emotional, and personality development* (5th ed., pp. 1051–1071). New York: John Wiley & Sons.

Echols, L.D., West, R.F., Stanovich, K.E., & Zehr, K.S. (1996). Using children's literacy activities to predict growth in verbal cognitive skills: A longitudinal investigation. *Journal of Educational Psychology, 88*(2), 296–304.

Everitt, B.S., Landau, S., & Leese, M. (2001). *Cluster analysis* (4th ed.). London: Edward Arnold.

Francis, B. (1999). Lads, lasses and (new) labour: 14–16-year-old students' responses to the 'laddish behaviour and boys' underachievement' debate. *British Journal of Sociology of Education, 20*(3), 355-371.

Fredricks, J., Blumenfeld, P., & Paris, A. (2004). School engagement: Potential of the concept, state of the evidence. *Review of Educational Research, 74,* 59–109.

Freebody, P., & Anderson, R.C. (1983). Effects on text comprehension of differing proportions and locations of difficult vocabulary. *Journal of Reading Behavior, 15*(3), 19–39.

Fuchs, L.S., Fuchs, D., Hosp, M.K., & Jenkins, J.R. (2001). Oral reading fluency as an indicator of reading competence: A theoretical, empirical, and historical analysis. *Scientific Studies of Reading, 5*(3), 239–256.

Garnier, H.E., Stein, J.A., & Jacobs, J.K. (1997). The process of dropping out of high school: A 19-year perspective. *American Educational Research Journal, 34*(2), 395–419.

Gottfried, A.E. (1982). Relationships between academic intrinsic motivation and anxiety in children and young adolescents. *Journal of School Psychology, 20*(3), 205–215.

Gottfried, A.E. (1985). Academic intrinsic motivation in elementary and junior high school students. *Journal of Educational Psychology, 77*(6), 631–645.

Gottfried, A.E. (1990). Academic intrinsic motivation in young elementary school children. *Journal of Educational Psychology, 82*(3), 525–538.

Grolnick, W.S., Ryan, R.M., & Deci, E.L. (1991). Inner resources for school achievement: Motivational mediators of children's perceptions of their parents. *Journal of Educational Psychology, 83,* 508–517.

Gurian, M., & Henley, P. (2001). *Boys and girls learn differently! A guide for teachers and parents.* San Francisco: Jossey-Bass.

Guthrie, J.T., Meter, P.V., McCann, A.D., Wigfield, A., Bennett, L., Poundstone, C.C., et al. (1996). Growth of literacy engagement: Changes in motivations and strategies during Concept-Oriented Reading Instruction. *Reading Research Quarterly, 31*(3), 306–332.

Guthrie, J.T., Wigfield, A., Metsala, J.L., & Cox, K.E. (1999). Motivational and cognitive predictors of text comprehension and reading amount. *Scientific Studies of Reading, 3*(3), 231–256.

Guthrie, J.T., Wigfield, A., & VonSecker, C. (2000). Effects of integrated instruction on motivation and strategy use in reading. *Journal of Educational Psychology, 92*(2), 331–341.

Hao, L., & Cherlin, A.J. (2004). Welfare reform and teenage pregnancy, childbirth, and school dropout. *Journal of Marriage and Family, 66*(1), 179–194.

Hart, B., & Risley, T.R. (1995). *Meaningful differences in the everyday experience of young American children.* Baltimore: Paul H. Brookes Publishing Co.

Harter, S. (1981). A new self–report scale of intrinsic versus extrinsic orientation in the classroom: Motivational and informational components. *Developmental Psychology, 17,* 300–312.

Harter, S. (1985a). *Self-Perception Profile for Children.* Denver, CO: University of Denver.

Harter, S. (1985b). *Social Support Scale for Children.* Denver, CO: University of Denver.

Harter, S. (1988). *Self-Perception Profile for Adolescents.* CO: University of Denver.

Harter, S. (1993). Causes and consequences of low self-esteem in children and adolescents. In R.F. Baumeister (Ed.), *Self-esteem: The puzzle of low self regard* (pp. 87–116). New York: Kluwer Academic/Plenum.

Harter, S., & Connell, J.P. (1984). A model of children' s achievement and related self-perceptions of competence, control and motivational orientation. In J. Nicholls (Ed.), *Advances in motivation and achievement* (pp. 219–250). Greenwich, CT: JAI Press.

Hightower, A.D., Work, W.C., Cowen, E.L., Lotyczewski, B.S., Spinell, A.P., Guare, J.C., et al. (1986). The Teacher-Child Rating Scale: A brief objective measure of elementary children's school problem behaviors and competencies. *School Psychology Review, 15*(3), 393–409.

Hoff-Ginsberg, E., & Tardif, T. (1995). Socioeconomic status and parenting. In M.H. Bornstein (Ed.), *Handbook of parenting, Vol. 2: Biology and ecology of parenting* (pp. 161–188). Mahwah, NJ: Lawrence Erlbaum Associates.

Holmbeck, G.N., Paikoff, R.L., & Brooks-Gunn, J. (1995). Parenting adolescents. In M.H. Bornstein (Ed.), *Handbook of parenting, Vol. 1: Children and parenting.* (pp. 91–118): Lawrence Erlbaum Associates, Inc.

Holy Bible, King James Version. Matthew XXV:29.

Hoover, W.A., & Gough, P.B. (1990). The simple view of reading. *Reading and Writing: An Interdisciplinary Journal, 2*(2), 127–160.

Jackson, C. (2002). "Laddishness" as a self-worth protection strategy. *Gender and Education, 14*(1), 37–51.

Jastak, S., & Wilkinson, G. (1984). *The Wide Range Achievement Test–Revised.* Wilmington, DE: Jastak Associates.

Jordan, G.E., Snow, C.E., & Porche, M.V. (2000). Project EASE: The effect of a family literacy project on kindergarten students' early literacy skills. *Reading Research Quarterly, 35*(4), 524–546.

Katz, J.R. (2001). Playing at home: The talk of pretend play. In D.K. Dickinson & P.O. Tabors (Eds.), *Beginning literacy with language: Young children learning at home and school* (pp. 53–73). Baltimore: Paul H. Brookes Publishing Co.

Kimmel, M.S. (2000). *The gendered society.* New York: Oxford University Press.

Kurland, B.F., & Snow, C.E. (1997). Longitudinal measurement of growth in definitional skill. *Journal of Child Language, 24*(3), 603–625.

Lareau, A., & Horvat, E.M. (1999). Moments of social inclusion and exclusion: Race, class, and cultural capital in family-school relationships. *Sociology of Education, 72*(1), 37-53.

Lashaway-Bokina, N. (2000). Recognizing and nurturing intrinsic motivation: A cautionary tale. *Roeper Review, 22*(4), 225–227.

Lee, V.E., & Burkam, D.T. (2003). Dropping out of high school: The role of school organization and structure. *American Educational Research Journal, 40*(2), 353–393.

Lee, V. E., & Loeb, S. (2000). School size in Chicago elementary schools: Effects on teachers' attitudes and students' achievement. *American Educational Research Journal, 37*(1), 3-31.

Lee, V.E., & Smith, J.B. (1997). High school size: Which works best and for whom? *Educational Evaluation and Policy Analysis, 19*(3), 205–227.

Lemke, M., Lippman, L., Bairu, G., Calsyn, C., Kruger, T., Jocelyn, L., et al. (2001). *Outcomes of learning: Results from the 2000 Program for International Student Assessment of 15-Year-Olds in Reading, Mathematics, and Science Literacy.* Washington, DC: U.S. Department of Education, National Center for Education Statistics..

Lloyd, J., & Barenblatt, L. (1984). Intrinsic intellectuality: Its relations to social class, intelligence, and achievement. *Journal of Personality and Social Psychology, 46,* 646–654.

Losen, D.J. (2004). Graduation rate accountability under the No Child Left Behind Act and the disparate impact on students of color. In G. Orfield (Ed.), *Dropouts in America: Confronting the graduation rate crisis* (pp. 41–56). Cambridge, MA: Harvard Education Press.

Marks, C.B., Doctorow, M.J., & Wittrock, M.C. (1974). Word frequency and reading comprehension. *Journal of Educational Research, 67*(6), 259–262.

Martin, A.J., Marsh, H.W., & Debus, R.L. (2001). Self-handicapping and defensive pessimism: Exploring a model of predictors and outcomes from a self-protection perspective. *Journal of Educational Psychology, 93*(1), 87–102.

Mason, J. (1992). Reading stories to preliterate children: A proposed connection to reading. In P. Gough, L. Ehri & R. Treiman (Eds.), *Reading acquisition* (pp. 215–243). Hillsdale, NJ: Lawrence Erlbaum Associates.

Mason, J., & Stewart, J. (1989). *Early Childhood Diagnostic Instrument: The Comprehensive Assessment Program.* Iowa City, IA: American Testronics.

Masten, A.S. (2001). Ordinary magic: Resilience processes in development. *American Psychologist, 56*(3), 227–238.

Masten, A.S., Hubbard, J.J., Gest, S.D., Tellegen, A., Garmezy, N., & Ramirez, M. (1999). Competence in the context of adversity: Pathways to resilience and maladaptation from childhood to late adolescence. *Development and Psychopathology, 11,* 143–169.

McGee, L.M., & Richgels, D.J. (2003). *Designing early literacy programs: Strategies for at-risk preschool and kindergarten children.* New York: Guilford Press.

McKenna, M.C., Kear, D.J., & Ellsworth, R.A. (1995). Children's attitudes toward reading: A national survey. *Reading Research Quarterly, 30*(4), 934–956.

McKeown, M.G., Beck, I.L., Omanson, R., & Perfetti, C.A. (1983). The effects of long-term vocabulary instruction on reading comprehension: A replication. *Journal of Reading Behavior, 15*(1), 3–18.

McLoyd, V.C. (1998). Socioeconomic disadvantage and child development. *American Psychologist, 53*(2), 185–204.

Midgley, C., Anderman, E.M., & Hicks, L. (1995). Differences between elementary and middle school teachers and students: A goal theory approach. *Journal of Early Adolescence, 15*(1), 90–113.

Miller, J. (1981). *Assessing language disorders in children.* Baltimore: University Park Press.

Moje, E. B. (2006). Motivating texts, motivating contexts, motivating adolescents: An examination of the role of motivation in adolescent literacy practices and development. *Perspectives, 32*(3), 10–14.

Monkman, K., Ronald, M., & Theramene, F.D. (2005). Social and cultural capital in an urban Latino school community. *Urban Education, 40*(1), 4–33.

Mullen, C.A. (2002). The original ten: A multisite case study of Florida's Millennium High School reform model. *Education Policy Analysis Archives, 10*(40).

Murnane, R.J., & Levy, F. (1996). *Teaching the new basic skills: Principles for educating children to thrive in a changing economy.* New York: Kessler Books.

Nagy, W.E., & Herman, P.A. (1985). Incidental vs. instructional approaches to increasing reading vocabulary. *Educational Perspectives, 23*(1), 16–21.

Nathan, R. G., & Stanovich, K. E. (1991). The causes and consequences of differences in reading fluency. *Theory into Practice, 30*(3), 176–184.

Nation, K., & Snowling, M.J. (1998). Individual differences in contextual facilitation: Evidence from dyslexia and poor reading comprehension. *Child Development, 69*(4), 996–1011.

National Center for Education Statistics. (1996). *NAEP 1994 reading report card for the nation and the states: Findings from the National Assessment of Educational Progress and Trial State Assessment.* Washington, DC: Office of Educational Research and Improvement, U.S. Department of Education.

National Center for Education Statistics. (2001). *Dropout rates in the United States: 2000, NCES 2002-114.* Washington, DC: U.S. Department of Education.

National Center for Education Statistics. (2003). *The nation's report card: Reading highlights 2003.* Washington, DC: Office of Educational Research and Improvement, U.S. Department of Education.

National Center for Education Statistics. (2005). *NEAP 2004 trends in academic progress: Three decades of student performance in reading and mathematics (NCES 2005-464).* Washington, DC: Institute of Education Sciences, U.S. Department of Education.

National Center for Education Statistics. (2006). National trends in reading by performance levels. Retrieved November 21, 2006, from http://nces.ed.gov/nationsreportcard/ltt/results2004/nat-reading-perf.asp

National Reading Panel. (2000). *Teaching children to read: An evidence-based assessment of the scientific research literature on reading and its implications for reading instruction.* Washington, DC: National Institute of Child Health and Human Development.

Nayak, A. (2003). 'Boyz to Men': Masculinities, schooling and labour transitions in de-industrial times. *Educational Review, 55*(2), 147–159.

Nelson, P.S., Simoni, J.M., & Adelman, H.S. (1996). Mobility and school functioning in the early grades. *Journal of Educational Research, 89*(6), 365–369.

No Child Left Behind Act of 2001, PL 107-110, 115 Stat. 1425, 20 U.S.C. §§ 6301 *et seq.*

Noguera, P.A. (2002). Beyond size: The challenge of high school reform. *Educational Leadership, 59*(5), 60–63.

Noguera, P. A., & Wing, J. Y. (Eds.). (2006). *Unfinished business: Closing the racial achievement gap in our schools.* San Francisco: Jossey-Bass.

Nottelmann, E.D. (1987). Competence and self-esteem during the transition from childhood to adolescence. *Developmental Psychology, 23*(3), 441–450.

Orfield, G. (Ed.). (2004). *Dropouts in America: Confronting the graduation rate crisis.* Cambridge, MA: Harvard Education Press.

Organization for Economic Co-Operation and Development (OECD). (2001). Knowledge and skills for life: First results from the OECD Programme for International Student Assessment (PISA) 2000. from http://www.pisa.oecd.org/dataoecd/44/53/33691596.pdf

Patrick, B.C., Skinner, E.A., & Connell, J.P. (1993). What motivates children's behavior and emotion? The joint effects of perceived control and autonomy in the academic domain. *Journal of Personality and Social Psychology, 65*(4), 781–791.

Perie, M., Grigg, W., and Donahue, P. (2005). *The nation's report card: Reading 2005* (NCES 2006–451). U.S. Department of Education, National Center for Education Statistics. Washington, D.C.: U.S. Government Printing Office.

Perie, M., Moran, R., & Lutkus, A.D. (2005). *NAEP 2004 trends in academic progress: Three decades of student performance in reading and mathematics.* (NCES 2005–464). U.S. Department of Education, Institute of Education Sciences, National Center for Education Statistics. Washington, DC: Government Printing Office.

Pianta, R.C., & Walsh, D.J. (1996). *High-risk children in schools: Constructing sustaining relationships.* New York: Routledge.

Popplewell, S.R., & Doty, D.E. (2001). Classroom instruction and reading comprehension: A comparison of one basal reader approach and the Four-Blocks framework. *Reading Psychology, 22*(2), 83–94.

Porche, M.V., & Ross, S.J. (2003). *Academic success and struggle: A study of motivation and literacy in a sample of low-income 7th graders.* Wellesley, MA: Wellesley Centers for Women Working Paper No. 410.

Porche, M.V., Ross, S.J., & Snow, C.E. (2004). From preschool to middle-school: The role of masculinity in low-income urban adolescent boys' literacy skills and academic achievement. In N. Way & J. Chu (Eds.), *Adolescent boys: Exploring diverse cultures of boyhood* (pp. 338–360). New York: New York University Press.

Public Law 107–110. No child left behind act of 2001. Retrieved from http://www.ed.gov/policy/elsec/leg/esea02/107-110.pdf

Purcell-Gates, V. (1996). Stories, coupons, and the "TV Guide": Relationships between home literacy experiences and emergent literacy knowledge. *Reading Research Quarterly, 31*(4), 406–428.

Raider-Roth, M. (2005). *Trusting what you know: The high stakes of classroom relationships.* San Francisco: Jossey-Bass.

RAND Reading Study Group. (2002). *Reading for understanding: Toward an R&D program in reading comprehension.* Santa Monica, CA: RAND Corporation.

Rathbun, A., & West, J. (2004). *From kindergarten through third grade: Children's beginning school experiences.* (NCES 2004–007).U.S. Department of Education, National Center for Education Statistics. Washington, DC: U.S. Government Printing Office.

Reed, D.F., McMillan, J.H., & McBee, R.H. (1995). Defying the odds: Middle schoolers in high risk circumstances who succeed. *Middle School Journal, 27*(1), 3–10.

Roderick, M. (2003). What's happening to the boys? Early high school experiences and school outcomes among African American male adolescents in Chicago. *Urban Education, 38*(5), 538–607.

Roderick, M., & Camburn, E. (1999). Risk and recovery from course failure in the early years of high school. *American Educational Research Journal, 36*(2), 303–343.

Roeser, R.W., & Eccles, J.S. (1998). Adolescents' perceptions of middle school: Relation to longitudinal changes in academic and psychological adjustment. *Journal of Research on Adolescence, 8*(1), 123–158.

Roeser, R.W., Eccles, J.S., & Sameroff, A. J. (2000). School as a context of early adolescents' academic and social-emotional development: A summary of research findings. *Elementary School Journal, 100*(5), 443–471.

Ross, S.J., Roach, K., & Tabors, P.O. (2000). *Motivational resources, teachers' perceptions, and academic achievement among low-income 6th and 7th graders.* Paper presented at the American Educational Research Association Annual Meeting, New Orleans, LA.

Rothstein, R. (2004). *Class and schools: Using social, economic, and educational reform to close the Black-white achievement gap.* Washington, DC: Economic Policy Institute.

Ryan, R.M., & Connell, J.P. (1989). Perceived locus of causality and internalization: Examining reasons for acting in two domains. *Journal of Personality and Social Psychology, 57,* 749–761.

Scarborough, H.S. (2001). Connecting early language and literacy to later reading (dis)abilities: Evidence, theory, and practice. In S. Neuman & D. Dickinson (Eds.), *Handbook of early literacy research.* (pp. 97–110). New York: Guilford Press.

Scarborough, H.S., Dobrich, W., & Hager, M. (1991). Literacy experience and reading disability: Reading habits and abilities of parents and young children. *Journal of Learning Disabilities, 24,* 508–511.

Schoenbach, R., Greenleaf, C., Cziko, C., & Hurwitz, L. (1999). *Reading for understanding: A guide to improving reading in middle and high school classrooms.* San Francisco: Jossey-Bass.

Scholz, R.W., & Tietje, O. (2001). *Embedded case study methods : Integrating quantitative and qualitative knowledge.* Thousand Oaks, CA: Sage Publications.

Searle, S.R., Casella, G., & McCulloch, C.E. (1992). *Variance components.* New York: John Wiley & Sons, Inc.

Simmons, R.G., & Blyth, D.A. (1987). *Moving into adolescence: The impact of pubertal change and school context.* New York: Aldine de Gruyter.

Singer, J.D. (1998). Using SAS PROC MIXED to fit multilevel models, hierarchical models, and individual growth models. *Journal of Educational and Behavioral Statistics, 24*(4), 323–355.

Singer, J.D., & Willett, J.B. (2003). *Applied longitudinal data analysis: Modeling change and event occurrence.* New York: Oxford University Press.

Sivan, E. (1986). Motivation in social constructivist theory. *Educational Psychologist, 21,* 209–233.

Smith, M.W. (2001). Children's experiences in preschool. In D.K. Dickinson & P.O. Tabors (Eds.), *Beginning literacy with language: Young children learning at home and school* (pp. 149–174). Baltimore: Paul H. Brookes Publishing Co.

Snow, C.E. (1990). The development of definitional skill. *Journal of Child Language, 17*(3), 697–710.

Snow, C.E., Barnes, W.S., Chandler, J., Hemphill, L., & Goodman, I.F. (1991). *Unfulfilled expectations: Home and school influences on literacy.* Cambridge, MA: Harvard University Press.

Snow, C.E., Burns, S., & Griffin, P. (Eds.). (1998). *Preventing reading difficulties in young children.* Washington, DC: National Academy Press.

Snow, C.E., & Dickinson, D.K. (1990). Social sources of narrative skills at home and at school. *First Language, 10,* 87–103.

Snow, C.E., & Dickinson, D.K. (1991). Some skills that aren't basic in a new conception of literacy. In A. Purves & T. Jennings (Eds.), *Literate systems and individual lives: Perspectives on literacy and schooling* (pp. 175–213). Albany, NY: SUNY Press.

Snow, C.E., Tabors, P.O., & Dickinson, D.K. (2001). Language development in the preschool years. In D.K. Dickinson & P.O. Tabors (Eds.), *Beginning literacy with language: Young children learning at home and school* (pp. 1–25). Baltimore: Paul H. Brookes Publishing Co.

Snow, C.E., Tabors, P.O., Nicholson, P.A., & Kurland, B.F. (1995). SHELL: Oral language and early literacy skills in kindergarten and first-grade children. *Journal of Research in Childhood Education, 10*(1), 37–48.

Stahl, S.A. (2003). Words are learned incrementally over multiple exposures. *American Educator, Spring,* 18–19.

Stahl, S.A., & Fairbanks, M.M. (1986). The effects of vocabulary instruction: A model-based meta-analysis. *Review of Educational Research, 56*(1), 72–110.

Stanovich, K.E. (1986). Matthew Effects in reading: Some consequences of individual differences in the acquisition of literacy. *Reading Research Quarterly, 21*(4), 360–407.

Stanovich, K.E. (1991). The psychology of reading: Evolutionary and revolutionary developments. *Annual Review of Applied Linguistics, 12,* 3–30.

Stanovich, K.E., Nathan, R.G., & Zolman, J.E. (1988). The developmental lag hypothesis in reading: Longitudinal and matched reading-level comparisons. *Child Development, 59*(1), 71–86.

Stanovich, K.E., West, R.F., Cunningham, A.E., Cipielewski, J., & Siddiqui, S. (1996). The role of inadequate print exposure as a determinant of reading comprehension problems. In C. Cornoldi & J. Oakhill (Eds.), *Reading comprehension disabilities: Processes and intervention* (pp. 15–32). Mahwah, NJ: Lawrence Erlbaum Associates.

Stanovich, K.E., West, R.F., & Harrison, M.R. (1995). Knowledge growth and maintenance across the life span: The role of print exposure. *Developmental Psychology, 31*(5), 811–826.

Stein, N., Tolman, D.L., Porche, M.V., & Spencer, R. (2002). Gender safety: A new concept for safer and more equitable schools. *Journal of School Violence, 1*(2), 35–49.

Sternberg, R.J. (1987). Most vocabulary is learned from context. In M.G. McKeown & M.E. Curtis (Eds.), *The nature of vocabulary acquisition* (pp. 89–106). Hillsdale, NJ: Lawrence Erlbaum Associates.

Storch, S.A., & Whitehurst, G.J. (2002). Oral language and code-related precursors to reading: Evidence from a longitudinal structural model. *Developmental Psychology, 38*(6), 934–947.

Sweet, A.P., Guthrie, J.T., & Ng, M.M. (1998). Teacher perceptions and student reading motivation. *Journal of Educational Psychology, 90*(2), 210–223.

Tabors, P.O., Beals, D.E., & Weizman, Z.O. (2001). "You know what oxygen is?": Learning new words at home. In D.K. Dickinson & P.O. Tabors (Eds.), *Beginning literacy with language: Young children learning at home and school* (pp. 93–110). Baltimore: Paul H. Brookes Publishing Co.

Tabors, P.O., Roach, K.A., & Snow, C.E. (2001). Home language and literacy environment: Final results. In D.K. Dickinson & P.O. Tabors (Eds.), *Beginning literacy with lan-*

guage: Young children learning at home and school (pp. 111–138). Baltimore: Paul H. Brookes Publishing Co.

Tabors, P.O., Snow, C.E., & Dickinson, D.K. (2001). Homes and schools together: Supporting language and literacy development. In D.K. Dickinson & P.O. Tabors (Eds.), *Beginning literacy with language: Young children learning at home and school* (pp. 313–334). Baltimore: Paul H. Brookes Publishing Co.

Taylor, B.M., Pearson, P.D., Peterson, D.S., & Rodriguez, M.C. (2003). Reading growth in high-poverty classrooms: The influence of teacher practices that encourage cognitive engagement in literacy learning. *Elementary School Journal, 104*(1), 3–28.

Thompson, F.T. (2002). Student achievement, selected environmental characteristics, and neighborhood type. *Urban Review, 34*(3), 277–292.

Topping, K., Valtin, R., Roller, C., Brozo, W., & Dionisio, M.L. (2003). *Policy and practice implications of the Program for International Student Assessment (PISA) 2000. Report of the International Reading Association PISA Task Force.* Newark, DE: International Reading Association.

Toutkoushian, R.K., & Curtis, T. (2005). Effects of socioeconomic factors on public high school outcomes and rankings. *Journal of Educational Research, 98*(5), 259–271.

Vander Ark, T.V. (2002). The case for small high schools. *Educational Leadership, 59*(5), 55–59.

Vaishnav, A. (2004, April 6). High school dropout rates are up sharply. *The Boston Globe.* p. B3.

Velasco, P.M. (1989). *The relationship of oral decontextualized language and reading comprehension in bilingual children.* Cambridge, MA: Harvard University.

Vellutino, F.R. (2003). Individual differences as sources of variability in reading comprehension in elementary school children. In A.P. Sweet & C.E. Snow (Eds.), *Rethinking reading comprehension* (pp. 51–81). New York: Guilford Press.

Vellutino, F.R., & Scanlon, D.M. (2002). The interactive strategies approach to reading intervention. *Contemporary Educational Psychology, 27,* 573–635.

Vellutino, F.R., Scanlon, D.M., & Tanzman, M.S. (1994). Components of reading ability: Issues and problems in operationalizing word identification, phonological coding, and orthographic coding. In G.R. Lyon (Ed.), *Frames of reference for the assessment of learning disabilities: New views on measurement issues* (pp. 279–332). Baltimore: Paul H. Brookes Publishing Co.

Verdugo, R.R. (2002). Race-ethnicity, social class, and zero-tolerance policies: The cultural and structural wars. *Education and Urban Society, 35*(1), 50–75.

Walker, D., Greenwood, C., Hart, B., & Carta, J. (1994). Prediction of school outcomes based on early language production and socioeconomic factors. *Child Development, 65*(2 Apr), 606–621.

West, J., Denton, K., & Reaney, L. (2000). *The kindergarten year: Findings from the Early Childhood Longitudinal Study, Kindergarten Class of 1998–99.* (NCES 2001023). U.S. Department of Education, National Center for Education Statistics. Washington, DC: U.S. Government Printing Office.

Whitehurst, G.J. (1997). Language processes in context: Language learning in children reared in poverty. In L.B. Adamson & M.A. Romski (Eds.), *Research on communication and language disorders: Contributions to theories of language development* (pp. 233–266). Baltimore: Paul H. Brookes Publishing Co.

Whitehurst, G.J., & Lonigan, C.J. (1998). Child development and emergent literacy. *Child Development, 69*(3), 848–872.

Wigfield, A. (1997). Reading motivation: A domain-specific approach to motivation. *Educational Psychologist, 32,* 59–68.

Wigfield, A., & Aster, S. (1984). Social and motivational influences on reading. In P.D. Pearson (Ed.), *Handbook of reading research.* New York: Longman.

Wigfield, A., & Eccles, J.S. (1992). The development of achievement task values: A theoretical analysis. *Developmental Review, 12,* 265–310.

Wigfield, A., Eccles, J.S., Mac Iver, D., Reuman, D.A., & Midgley, C. (1991). Transitions during early adolescence: Changes in children's domain-specific self-perceptions and general self-esteem across the transition to junior high school. *Developmental Psychology, 27*(4), 552–565.

Wigfield, A., & Guthrie, J.T. (1997). Relations of children's motivation for reading to the amount and breadth of their reading. *Journal of Educational Psychology, 89*(3), 420–432.

Wigfield, A., & Harold, R. (1992). Teacher beliefs and children's achievement self-perceptions: A developmental perspective. In D. Schunk & J. Meece (Eds.), *Student perceptions in the classroom* (pp. 95–121). Mahwah, NJ: Lawrence Erlbaum Associates.

Willis, P. (1977). *Learning to labour: How working class kids get working class jobs.* Farnborough, England: Saxon House.

Wolf, M., & Katzir-Cohen, T. (2001). Reading fluency and its intervention. *Scientific Studies of Reading, 5*(3), 211–238.

Woods, M.L., & Moe, A.J. (1989). *Analytical reading inventory* (4th ed.). New York: Macmillan.

Index

Page numbers followed by *f*, t, and *n* indicate figures, tables, and footnotes respectively.